About the Author

John Blackman was born in Melbourne in 1947 and began his showbusiness career in 1969. Since then he has become well-known through radio shows on 2CA, 2GN, 2UE, 2GB, 3AW, 3AK and 3UZ.

However, he is best-known to millions of Australians as 'the voice' of the highly successful, anarchic, ad-lib, weekly variety show 'Hey Hey It's Saturday'. Blackman and his alter ego, Dickie Knee, have been an integral part of the show since its inception 24 years ago.

Blackman lives in Melbourne with his wife and 20-year-old daughter.

Also by John Blackman in Sun

The Aussie Slang Dictionary
Don't Come the Raw Prawn

JOHN BLACKMAN'S

BEST OF
AUSSIE SLANG

Sun

Pan Macmillan Australia

First published 1995 in Sun by Pan Macmillan Australia Pty Limited
St Martins Tower, 31 Market Street, Sydney

National Library of Australia
cataloguing-in-publication data:

Blackman, John, 1947– .
John Blackman's best of Aussie slang.

ISBN 0 7251 0746 4.

1. English language – Australia – Slang. I. Title.

427.994

Typeset in 12/13pt Officina Sans by Midland Typesetters
Printed by Australian Print Group, Maryborough, Vic.

A Word From John Blackman

To be quite honest, I am a little embarrassed to be writing this foreword.

You see, after my first foray into the literary world sold and re-printed and my subsequent effort did the same—both to my amazement—my publishers dubbed me with the rather flattering epithet of becoming one of their 'preferred authors'.

I say embarrassed because there are many more talented, qualified, intellectual, hard-working, legitimate authors who not only deserve the aforementioned status but should not have to share the literary stage with jumped-up Johnnies like me. In fact, I was absent the day they did English expression at Syndal Tech!

Anyway, enough of this self-effacement—here is the result of my latest toil.

Purists and scholars of the English language may not only find some (indeed many) words and phrases missing but (and quite rightly) could dispute the origins of same.

Indeed, the Australian/English/American vernacular has become such an amalgam over recent years (due to more sophisticated communication) that true accuracy is extremely hard to maintain and would only bog us down in boring detail, make the book two inches thick and far too expensive!

That notwithstanding, the writer has made every attempt to thoroughly research each and every word and phrase and, although not the quintessential reference guide to our quirky colloquialisms (try saying that five times quickly after a skinful) it contains most of the phrases and words you will hear on any day anywhere in Australia.

Again, where words are inadequate, talented young cartoonist Andrew Fyfe has let his mind run rife with illustrations featuring a chap bearing an uncanny resemblance to the author (public ridicule and contempt charges still pending).

So here it is—just in time for the Sydney 2000 Olympics! JOHN BLACKMAN'S BEST OF AUSSIE SLANG . . . ta dah!

The ideal gift for that hard-to-buy-for relative, friend or overseas business associate. Whoever it is, I'm sure they will find a special place for my latest literary triumph—preferably one that doesn't flush!

Happy reading.

TO PUT THE ACID ON

A

To dismiss someone out-of-hand is to give them the 'big A'. It's a more polite way of saying you've given something or someone the arse. People who are dismissed from their jobs are said to have been given 'the arse' or 'Tijuana'—rhyming slang for Tijuana Brass.

acid, to put the . . . on

To ply someone for either help, money or sex. (As I get older, I need help with all three!)

acre

Your backside, bum, arse, ass, bottom et al. Nirvana for a lot of Aussies is sitting on your acre doing nothing but watching the grass grow.

act the goat

To behave in a silly or foolish manner.

Adrians

Abbreviation of Adrian Quist (noted tennis player) and rhyming slang for 'pissed' or drunk. 'How drunk? He woke up the next morning and found his clothes scattered all over the front lawn . . . problem was he was still wearing them!'

TO ACT THE GOAT

aerial ping-pong
Derogatory term used to describe the football game of Aussie Rules by fans of cross-country wrestling (derogatory term used by Aussie Rules fans to describe rugby).

aggro
Abbreviation of 'aggravation'. It can describe an angry, belligerent person or trouble as in 'Don't give me any aggro'. It's also the name of an obnoxious (but very funny) little puppet seen frequently on Australian television.

airs
Abbreviation of the phrase 'airs and graces'. Just a little pretentious . . . Pretentious. Moi?

airy
What happens when you take a swing at golf and miss (air swing) and what most blokes' (and some sheilas') armpits are . . . sorry about that one!

airy-fairy
Something of very little substance. E.g. a political party's policies.

Akubra
Our very distinctive broad-brimmed Australian bush hat made from rabbit fur. Worn in the main by the man-on-the-land, Greg Norman and occasionally by wankers in the city!

AGGRO

Al Capone

Rhyming slang for telephone. Also 'dog and bone' and 'eau de Cologne'. In Australia, we often give each other a gin sling (ring) on the dog!

aleck

There are two types of this person. A smart aleck who seems to know everything but generally knows stuff-all or a person of limited intellectual capacity who spends most of his life achieving very little (alecking around).

Alice, the

Abbreviation for Alice Springs, a small town in the Northern Territory not far from that other great Aussie landmark, Ayers Rock, the world's largest monolith.

alkie

Abbreviation for alcoholic. As Dean Martin once said, 'If you drink, don't drive—don't even putt!'

AKUBRA

alley
A marble (generally made from glass if you can figure that one out). Sometimes known as an agate. Agate is also a euphemism for testicle for the obvious reason. Cricketers often 'cop one in the agates' if they don't keep their eye on that rising ball . . . it certainly quietens them down for a minute or two!

all right
Phrase used to indicate that everything's okay. Occasionally pronounced 'orright' . . . all right?

ankle biter
A young child or, if you prefer, a rug rat.

ants' pants
Anything or anyone who is looking fabulous (and knows it) is said to be the ants' pants.

Anzac
An Aussie soldier (or digger). Acronym for a member of the Australian and New Zealand Army Corps.

apples, she'll be
Quaint expression of indeterminate origin indicating that everything will be okay.

ANKLE BITER

appro
Something that you are inspecting or trying out before you buy is said to be out on appro (approval). It's also my wife's nickname for me!

arf-a-mo
No, not the result of a nasty shaving accident. Expression used when asking someone to wait a moment. 'I'll be with you in 'arf a mo.'

aristotle
Rhyming slang for bottle—as one great drinker once said, 'I'd rather have a free bottle in front of me than a prefrontal lobotomy!'

arse (1)
Your buttocks, posterior, acre, dot, crack, anus, freckle, ring etc.

arse (2)
Uncanny good luck. More arse than class!

arse (3)
Lucky.

arse, given the (4)
To be fired.

SHE'LL BE APPLES!

arse, to give it the (5)
When something ceases to be of use, throw it out. (Husbands can also be given the arse.)

arse about, to (6)
To mess around with little or no purpose . . . that's why you were given the arse in the first place you dummy!

arse about face (7)
Back-to-front.

arse about tit (8)
Back to front again!

arse over tit (9)
How you finish up when you fall over arsing about!

arse beats class (10)
If you manage to get through life depending more on luck than ability.

Arthur or Martha, doesn't know if he's (or she's)
A very confused person. Mind you, in these days of sex-change operations it's very hard to tell. My wife got a job at a sex-change clinic—says it's great. She gets to meet so many new men and women!

ARSE OVER TiT

arty-farty

You see them everywhere . . . art galleries, the opera, concert halls. People who have absolutely no knowledge of the arts but like to look as though they have. (See also **wankers**).

arvo

Abbreviation for afternoon—'See youse this arvo!'

ashtray, as useful as an . . . on a motorbike

Something totally useless. About the same as tits on a bull and a mountain goat who's afraid of heights (or a chameleon that's stuck on green!).

DOESN'T KNOW iF HE'S ARTHUR OR MARTHA

Aussie

Short for Orstralian mate! Pronounced as 'ozzie' not 'oss-see' as many Americans tend to do.

Aussie Rules

A fast moving football game played mainly in Victoria, South Australia, Western Australia, Tasmania and the Northern Territory. The AFL (Australian Football League) grand final in Melbourne each September attracts almost 100,000 spectators. 'You bloody mug umpie!' . . . primitive Aussie footy chant.

Australian adjective, the great

Simply the best bloody word in the bloody world to describe every bloody thing from a bloody good time to a bloody awful time to a bloody good bloke to a bloody mongrel. Got the bloody idea . . . that's bloody good then! (Quite acceptable profanity in any bloody company really—even with the bloody Archbishop!)

Australian salute

The constant waving of one's hand to brush away the ever-present blowie (blow fly). Some say the reason we don't kill 'em is because they're almost our national bird!

ARTY FARTY

axe handle

Early unit of measurement. If a bloke is described as being ten axe handles across—be very polite to him. If a girl is described as having a bum that's the same—don't mention it!

ay?

Literally it means 'I beg your pardon?' You know, when you didn't quite catch what someone said. New Zealanders tend to use it as an exclamation . . . 'Gee we had a good time at the cricket, ay!'

BAG

backchat
> Answering back. Impertinence. As a kid, I was an expert at backchat . . . unfortunately for me my dad was an expert at back*hand*!

back-door bandit
> Euphemism for male homosexual.

back o'beyond
> Term used to describe any remote area of outback Australia.

back o'Bourke
> An outback town that actually exists. Where is it? Back o'beyond somewhere!

back up, to
> Come in again for a second helping of something—generally food.

back up, to get someone's
> To really annoy somebody . . . like your missus when you *don't* ask for a second helping!

bag
> A very unattractive woman . . . in fact so ugly, whenever she goes into a bank, the security cameras start throwing up film!

bag, the old
> Uncomplimentary but affectionate term for either your wife or mother. (God knows what they call *us* behind our backs!)

bagging
> If you have just been on the end of a bagging, you have just been severely criticised. Aussies are fond of bagging things just for the fun of it . . . sometimes known as knocking—we're good at that too!

bag of fruit
> Rhyming slang for a man's suit. Hey, nice threads—it's a shame someone's made them into such a terrible suit!

bags I go next
> Inane expression of the desire to be next in line for something.

bags, rough as
> Untidy, uncouth, unattractive to the gaze. We are talking mega-ugly here!

bag your head!
> Shut-up, get stuffed, be quiet, stick your head up a dead bear's bum etc.

BAG YOUR HEAD!

bald as a bandicoot
So bald in fact that on my passport, they have my hair colour down as invisible!

ball and chain, the
Given the Aussie male's zealous regard for his freedom, the ball and chain could only be his wife, of course! We have the perfect marriage—she goes her way and *I* go her way!

balls-up
If something goes terribly wrong, it's regarded as a balls-up . . . a very close relation to the cock-up, stuff-up or screw-up.

ball tearer
In the testicular sense, something really exciting that causes them to spasm slightly.

banana bender
Our affectionate term for an inhabitant of the state where most of our bananas grow, Queensland.

bananaland
Where the banana benders come from silly! Who could forget that great movie *King Kong Loses His Banana*!

bandicoot on a burnt ridge, like a
Alone, forlorn, despairing . . . a bit like me at an orgy. I hate orgies. I never know who to thank when it's over!

LIKE A BANDICOOT ON A BURNT RIDGE

banged-up

> In the pudding club, pregnant (see also ***up the duff***.). My mother screamed a lot when she had me—and that was just during conception!

bang-on

> Expression meaning exactly right or well done!

bangs like a dunny door in a gale

> Used to describe a female member (of the opposite sex!) who is rather indiscriminate with her sexual favours . . . in short, a nymphomaniac.

bar, you wouldn't have a . . . of him/her/it

> Having nothing to do whatsoever with him/her/it.

barbie

> What Americans like to call 'cook-outs'. I'm hopeless at barbequing . . . those stupid baked beans keep falling through the grill!

barge into

> To interrupt a conversation or arrive unannounced.

barney

> A fight or violent disagreement . . . nothing to do with *The Flintstones*. By the way, are Barney and Betty Rubble married in real life?

BARBIE

barrack

The *Little Oxford Dictionary* tells us barracking could be jeering, but to barrack for your favourite footy team in Australia is to shout encouragement. (In the U.S.A. they call it rooting for your team.) In Australia however, if you were found rooting in the bleachers, you'd probably be thrown in gaol as it's a form of fornication in these here parts!

bash (1)

A party or celebration. E.g. birthday bash.

bash (2)

To attack verbally. In Australia some favourite bashees include politicians (fair game), tall poppies, entrepreneurs, social climbers etc.

bash, give it a

To try one's hand at something. 'I'll give it a bash'. Indeed, I'm giving this book a bash! If it doesn't get bashed by the critics, I'll throw a book bash to celebrate.

bashing your brains out

Extreme thinking or studying. The hardest five years of my school life were Third Grade! (Boom boom!)

basket case

Anybody on the brink of mental exhaustion or collapse.

BASKET CASE

BAT AND BALL

bat

Yet another uncomplimentary way to describe an unattractive member of the fairer sex. How ugly? Her idea of birth control is getting undressed with the lights on!

bat and ball (1)

Rhyming slang for stall, as in when you bat and ball your car.

bat and ball (2)

When things don't go your way and you become petulant and depart, you are said to have 'picked up your bat and ball and gone home' (as in spoiling a game of cricket). (See also *spitting the dummy* and *chucking the Glo-Mesh into the shagpile*.)

batching

What us married blokes do when the missus is away visiting her mother. Derived from 'bachelor'.

bathers

Swimming trunks—you know, what bathers wear.

battlers

Honest, hard working folk who are the back-bone of any nation. In Australia we call them 'little Aussie battlers'.

B.B.Q.
Abbreviation of barbeque.

beak (1)
Your proboscis, your hooter, your snout. People say I have a very big one. Actually, it's not—my face is just too small.

beak (2)
Your Honour, Your Worship, Your Hugeness, Your Bigness—yes folks, it's a judge or magistrate. When appearing in court, you are said to be 'going up before the beak'.

bearded clam, spearing the
A male term for fornication which, in all decency, needs no further explanation!

beauty
Generally used as an exclamation of delight. Variations include beaut!, bewdy! and bewdy bottler!

beddy byes
Where we all go when it's time for 'nye nyes'. I told my wife I wanted to die in bed. She said, 'Again?'

beef bayonet
The male sexual organ. (See also *tummy banana*, *blue vein flute*, *junket trumpet*, oh yes, and penis!)

BEEF TO THE ANKLES

beef to the ankles
Very fat! So fat in fact that Australia Post has given him his own postcode!

bell
To give someone a bell is to literally ring them on the telephone. My wife spends so much time on ours, Telecom are thinking of putting her up for a sainthood!

belt
A punch or haste. E.g. 'I'm just going to belt around the corner to give that bloke who ran off with my wife a good belting.'

better half
Generally speaking, your wife. It's funny, they never call us *their* better half. In any case, I certainly know who wears the panties in my family!

bib and tucker
Used to describe quality clothing. 'He was decked out in his best bib and tucker.'

bible basher
Religious zealot. Personally, I think born again Christians are a bigger pain the *second* time around!

bib, stick your . . . in
Interfering when you're not wanted.

big girl's blouse
An effeminate male.

Big Island, the
Nothing to do with Hawaii—it's what Tasmanians call Australia.

big note
If you brag about yourself, you are said to be 'big noting'. (See also **wanking**!)

big sticks
What Aussies call goal posts. If you dob it through the big sticks, you've just kicked a goal . . . Also vague male reference to sexual intercourse.

bike, the town
Nearly every town has one of course—a promiscuous female . . . perhaps that's where the term 'throwing a leg over' came from!

BILLY

bikkie

Juvenile abbreviation of biscuit. Remember kids, 'thank you' is something you say to make Mum let go of it!

billiard, as sharp as a

Obviously not over-endowed with the old grey matter. Thinks Iran is the past tense of Iraq!

billy

A tin can with a wire handle used in the bush to boil water over a campfire. You can't beat a nice cup of billy tea!

billy lid

Rhyming slang for kid.

billy-oh

A mythical place you tell someone to go when they've annoyed you. 'Go to billy-oh!' Also, if you sit on a keg of gun powder, you could be blown to billy-oh.

bingle

Aussie expression for a car wreck. My wife ran into the back of a Mercedes the other day. What she didn't tell me was there was a Volkswagen in between!

bit, getting a
Euphemistic term for having regular sex.

bit of all right
Anything that is attractive or promising (generally a good-looking member of the opposite sex is said to have this quality!).

bite, the
Whenever somebody borrows money from you—they put the bite on you. Personally I never lend money—it causes a disease called amnesia.

bitzer
A dog of mixed parentage—bitzer this and bitzer that. (See also *mongrel.*)

bizzo
Abbreviation of business. You will often hear an Aussie say he or she's got a bit of bizzo to do before the weekend.

black stump
Mythical, non-existent part of Australia in the middle of the continent. Oft heard expression: 'He's the best drover this side of the black stump!'

blazes, go to
Yet another non-existent mythical place you tell someone to go to when you're angry with them . . . it might have something to do with being a more polite way of telling somebody to go to hell. (See also *go to buggery.*)

blimey
An exclamation of amazement or surprise . . . if you're really surprised you may even say 'blimey teddy!' (Perhaps when confronted by a large bear?)

Bliss, Johnny
Nope, not an aging Aussie rock star but rhyming slang for piss (to urinate). It's particularly blissful if you've been hangin' on for a while!

block, to do your
Well, it could be something to do with your car but in fact, it's when you lose your temper—'block' being your head. (See also *chucking a wobbly/spaz.*)

bloke
General term for your average Aussie male. He could be a good bloke, a great bloke, a not a bad sort of bloke, or in my missus' case, a funny lookin' bloke.

bloke, like a . . . with boils on his arse
Let's face it, if you had to sit on them 24 hours a day you'd be a miserable, unhappy, complaining sort of bastard too!

bloody
Popularly known as the 'great Australian adjective', it can be used to express approval or disapproval. 'It's a bloody beautiful day' or 'It's a bloody awful day'—whichever bloody way you look at it, it's a bloody useful word!

bloody oath
Merely an extension of 'bloody' but expressing a more definite affirmation of something. 'Do you want another beer?', 'Bloody oath I do!'—sometimes shortened to 'blood oath'.

blow in
Any unexpected visitor is regarded a blow in, as in 'Look what the wind just blew in'.

blow off
Almost extinct expression for breaking wind. (Sometimes called air poos.)

blow through
If you leave town quickly without saying goodbye, paying any debts or at least offering to marry the poor girl, you are said to have blown through.

BLUDGE

bludge

To not do any work when you're supposed to is called 'having a bludge'. Bludgers come from all walks of life and are generally not highly regarded. Welfare recipients who make no effort whatsoever to seek work are known as dole bludgers—but still, at least when they get up each morning they know they're already *at* work!

blue (1)

Never accuse a dole bludger of being what he or she is 'cos you might end up in a blue. A blue (fight or argument) can be either physical (where your opponent beats the living crap out of you) or it can be an argument with your wife—personally, I'd sooner take the former every time!

Blue (2)

For some inexplicable reason, anyone who has red hair is referred to as 'Blue' in Australia. Two of the most popular comic strip characters were Bluey and Curly for many years both pre and post World War Two.

blue-arsed fly, running around like a

Anyone who is totally confused, running around hither and thither and achieving little or nothing whilst expending the maximum amount of effort is your typical blue-arsed fly.

blue swimmer

Our ten dollar note, so called due to its resemblance to the blue swimmer crab . . . the new plastic note also resembles our five dollar note—visitors beware!

blue vein flute

Euphemism for the penis—please don't ask me to go into detail—take a look next time you go for a Jimmy Bliss!

bluey (1)

A rolled up blanket containing a wandering bushman's (swaggie's) worldly possessions. To hump one's bluey is not a deviant sexual act. It's merely the act of walking around with it on your back . . . however what he does with it on those cold lonely nights in the bush is his business!

bluey (2)

A subpoena to make an appearance in court, so called as these summonses are generally printed on blue paper . . . when you get one, you are said to have 'copped a bluey'.

bob

Slang for our ten cent coin. Prior to the changeover to decimal currency in 1966, it was known as the shilling. Someone very rich is said to 'have a few bob'.

Bob's your uncle

Expression indicating you totally comprehend a situation. If someone doesn't believe you understand, they'll generally retort 'Yeah, and Fanny's your aunt!'

bodgie (1)

Fifties and sixties Aussie counterpart of the English teddy boy. Distinguishing features include greased-back hair, pointy-toed shoes, white socks, stove-pipe trousers and long sideburns. Some are still in existence today—but they're not a protected species!

bodgie (2)

Anything of dubious quality or origin is said to be bodgie. E.g. Never buy a television in a pub from a bloke who's out of breath—you can bet both are a bit bodgie!

bog, to go for a

To defecate—go for a Jimmy Britt (or even an Edgar Britt).

bog in, to

To get stuck into a meal. As that inspiring line of grace goes, 'Two, four, six, eight—bog in don't wait!' When I was a young tacker, Dad used to take care of Grace—until Mum caught them at it one night!

BODGIE

bollicles

Euphemism for testicles. English equivalent is bollocks. Something exciting or pleasing is sometimes said to be a 'tearer of bollicles'. (See also **ball tearer**.)

bollocky, in the

The state of being totally naked. I was arrested for streaking last year but got off—the evidence wouldn't stand up in court! . . . let's move on eh?

bolter

A long-priced winning race horse (a 'bolt from the blue'—or the back of the field). I can never figure out how a measly $2.00 bet can totally destroy a thoroughbred racehorse's will to win!

bomb

Any old car that barely runs—we had a bomb we called a 'Rolls Canardly' . . . rolls down the hills—can-hardly get up 'em!

bombers, brown or grey

Parking wardens from various states thus named because of the colour of their uniforms and the bombing raids they launch on your illegally parked car—not to mention your bank balance!

Bondi tram, to shoot through like a

To decamp rapidly, generally owing money and/or rent.

IN THE BOLLOCKY

boned up the bum

If you have been duped, you have just been boned. Not as painful as being boned up the bum without soap—now that can make the eyes water just a tad.

bone, to point the

Ancient Aboriginal ritual designed to cause a terminal case of death in the pointee. White folk use it as a term of accusation, but without the same dire consequences.

bonzer

Another great Aussie adjective (heard more in rural areas) to describe anything very pleasing. Take my missus, what a bonzer sheila! A bonzer bloke is said to be trustworthy and very good company.

boofhead

An idiot—you know, someone whose IQ matches his collar size! Oh yes, his head generally is a little over-sized as well.

boomerang, it's a

The utterly pathetic thing people say when you borrow something from them.

boot (1)

Something that happens to you when you get fired from your job.

BOOZE BUS

boot (2)

Aussie and British term for what Americans call their car 'trunk'.

boot, in yer

Mild, totally unexplainable expression of scorn or rejection.

boot, put the . . . in

To figuratively or physically kick someone when they're down.

booze bus

Mobile police van used to randomly breath test motorists. My mate crashed into one. The cop said, 'Didn't you see me?' My mate answered: 'I bloody hit ya didn't I!'

boozer (1)

Obviously, someone who does a lot of drinking.

boozer (2)

Is where they do their boozing—down the local boozer!

booze-up

A drunken revel—generally at the boozer with the rest of the boozers!

bo-peep

Nothing to do with that little girl and her sheep—it means to look. 'Take a bo-peep at the chick with those sheep man!'

BO-PEEP

bore it up 'em, to
To show the opposing team absolutely no mercy—especially satisfying when they have no hope of winning.

born in a tent, hey! were you . . .?
It's mandatory to use this expression to attack anybody who leaves a door open and lets in the cold air.

boss cocky
Used mainly in rural areas to signify the man in charge.

bot
This can either be a verb or adjective. To bot is to borrow something of little value with no intention of repaying the favour. If you indulge in this practice, you will be dubbed a 'bot'. American equivalent of bum.

bottle-oh!
Catch-cry of the roving beer bottle collector who, prior to our no-return, no-refund days, used to pay money to take away your empties. Our bottle-oh put his kids through university thanks to Dad's drinking problem!

bottler
Expression of delight—when your horse wins at 33/1 it's quite acceptable to scream, 'You bloody little bottler!'

bowyang
Not only surname of famous outback cartoon character—Ben Bowyang, but also the string of leather tied below the knees of bushmen's trousers—supposedly to stop snakes crawling up their legs and biting them on the family jewels!

box (1)
Vulgar expression for female genitalia.

box (2)
Sturdy plastic pouch cricketers wear down the front of their underpants to protect *their* genitalia.

bracket
Your backside . . . early form of childhood discipline—a foot up the bracket! Dad never did it to me—claimed it could cause brain damage!

brain, if he had another . . . it would be lonely
Scornful description of a dolt.

brains, not enough . . . to give him a headache
Same dope!

brasco
Slang term for toilet.

breadbasket
When a boxer (or anybody for that matter) gets whacked in the stomach, he's just copped one in the breadbasket.

break it down!
Similar exclamation to 'Oh come off it!' A demand for fair play.

brekkie
Yet another wonderful example of our penchant for shortening words and adding an 'ie'. If you deduced 'breakfast'—congrats! Help yourself to another poached googie (egg that is).

brick (1)
Formerly our ten pound note (now $20) so called due to its reddish hue.

BOWYANGS

brick (2)

If someone describes you as a real brick, you are regarded as a good, all round guy. Typical humorous retort is 'I thought he said *brick*!'

bride's nightie, up and down like a

Term used to describe anyone or thing that fluctuates wildly. (I thought he said fluctuate!)

brinny

Small flat pebble created by God for the specific purpose of skimming across water.

Britt, Jimmy

Rhyming slang for shit. Jimmy Britt was a former lightweight boxing champion who toured Australia during World War One. He has a non-existent cousin by the name of Edgar. So, whether you're going for a Jimmy or an Edgar, be sure to take a magazine with you and don't forget to wash your hands!

bronze, sitting on your

A phrase that requires little or no explanation. Your bronze—your backside, bum, dot, arse etc. I think we've got to the bottom of that!

brothel

In some states of Australia, they masquerade under the title of 'massage parlours'. It's also used to describe a dirty, untidy habitat. Often you will hear a mother scream, 'Clean up your room—it looks like a brothel!' My Mum still does it—and I'm nearly 47!

IT WOULD KILL A BROWN DOG

brown dog, it would kill a
Any food or beverage that is almost inedible . . . my wife served up a meatloaf with a hair in it—problem was it was still growing!

Bruce
With apologies to any red-blooded, heterosexual blokes called Bruce reading this—Bruce, uttered with plenty of sibilance, becomes a euphemism for a male homosexual.

bucket
To soundly criticise and/or find fault in something or somebody. Tipping a bucket on politicians is a favourite Aussie blood sport.

bucket of prawns, goes off like a . . . in the sun
This charming little phrase is used to describe a promiscuous woman willing to jump into bed at the drop of a hat . . . or a chequered flag for that matter!

Buckley's chance
Expression originating from Melbourne department store—Buckley and Nunn—to indicate futility. 'He's got two chances of winning the lottery—Buckley's . . . and none!'

buck's night
What Americans call a stag or bachelor party to initiate a bloke into marriage. I'll never forget my buck's night—the hotel manager still can't figure how we smuggled those 25 cheerleaders past the front desk!

bugger off
Expletive to indicate to someone you no longer require their company.

buggery, go to
Mythical place (we suspect similar to hell if that's all that goes on there) we tell people to bugger off to. Anything totally destroyed is also said to have been 'blown to buggery'.

bugle, on the
Something smelly or of dubious origins . . . take this book for instance.

bugs bunny
Rhyming slang for money.

bull

Anyone talking a load of rubbish is said to be 'talking a load of bull'. Cruder expressions are bullshit or bulldust—exponents of bullspeak are referred to as bullshit artists.

bull at a gate, like a

Tackling any task with impatience and no concern for the consequences.

bull, couldn't hit a . . . in the bum with a handful of wheat

Someone not blessed with good aim.

bullet

If you've just 'got the bullet' from your job, you've just been fired. They probably thought you weren't the right calibre anyway! (Oh my poor sides !!!)

bum

In America, he's a vagrant. It's also a verb associated with cadging a cigarette or a dollar from someone. In Australia, it's something we sit on!

bum, bite your

Very similar expression of scorn to 'in your boot'—but physically impossible.

bum freezer

You don't have to be a Rhodes Scholar to work this one out—it's a very short jacket!

BUM FREEZER

bunch of fives
If a bloke says he wants to give you a bunch of fives, he's not offering money but his fist . . . run like hell if he offers a bunch of tens!

bundle, dropped her
Rather uncomplimentary way of saying a woman has just whelped (er—given birth!).

bundle, dropped his
Someone who panics and loses control is said to have dropped his bundle.

bundy
Abbreviation for Bundaberg Rum from the Queensland town of the same name. Ideal mixed with Coke . . . after two or three, you can feel the intelligence draining from your entire body!

bung
Essentially this word means to simply 'put'. You may bung a few bucks on a horse, bung a dinner on the table, bung this book among your Tolstoys and Hemingways or you could bung me on the nose for having the temerity to even suggest it.

bung, gone
Generally applied to things mechanical when they no longer work—they've gone bung. (Can apply to brains as well!)

bunghole
A slang term for cheese . . . some varieties of which can bung up your hole in no uncertain manner.

bung, to . . . on side
To pretend to be a person of higher station than what you really are. (See also *airs* and *wankers*.)

bunny (1)
In our quaint game of cricket, the tailend batsmen (who are generally better at bowling). So called because of their ineptitude with the bat and their tendency to jump around dodging the fast deliveries.

bunny (2)
The Aussie equivalent of the American fall guy. If you're left holding the bag—you're the bunny!

burglar

Any golfer who plays better than his or her handicap in order to win money or the respect of fellow players. Lower than an amoeba on the food chain, these creatures must be exposed at every opportunity. I spend so much time in the bunkers at my club, they now call me Hitler!

Burke and Wills (1)

Rhyming slang for dills (idiots) . . . if there's just one of them—it's a Burke!

Burke and Wills, covered more ground than

In memory of Aussie trans-continental explorers from the last century, a term used to describe a horse that races all over the track.

burl

To give something a burl is to give something a try. You may give marriage a burl, a restaurant a burl or even take a car for a burl (test drive).

burn, to go for a

Very similar to 'burl' except in this it refers specifically to driving a car very fast . . . not too fast mind—or the cops might catch you and you could go for a row.

bushed (1)

Extremely lost.

bushed (2)

Extremely knackered (exhausted).

GO FOR A BURN

GET ALONG LIKE A BUSHFIRE

bushfire, to get along like a
To get on very well together. (See also *house on fire*.)

bushie
Anyone from out of town who hails from a rural area. (See also *bushwhacker*.)

bush lawyer
Anyone who gives unqualified, free and mostly unwelcome legal advice.

bushranger (1)
Distant cousin of the golfing burglar . . . at my club, I'm also known as Tarzan—I spend most of the game swinging from tree to tree!

bushranger (2)
Anyone who charges exorbitant fees . . . talking of my old accountant, a wise man once said, 'Never hire one that drives a bigger car than you do.'

bush telegraph
From the early days of Australia's settlement where informants would alert bushrangers (bandits) of approaching police. Modern day equivalent of the grapevine.

bush week, wadya think it is . . .?
Derisive retort aimed at someone who is blatantly trying to deceive or dupe you.

bushwhacker
Yet another rural type. (See also *bushie*.)

busier than a one-armed paper hanger/taxi driver with the crabs
This rather colourful, descriptive phrase is quite self-explanatory but reminds me of some graffiti I once saw in a public lavatory—'It's no good standing on the seat, the crabs in here jump six feet. It's no good going in next door—the crabs there jump six foot four!'

but
Word used to punctuate sentence. Common to only certain states—not Victoria but!

butchers (1)
Abbreviation of rhyming slang butcher's hook—or to feel a little crook (ill that is). So if an Aussie tells you he's feeling a bit butchers—stand back!

butchers (2)
Same abbreviation as above but this time it means to take a look. Typical usage: 'Take a butchers at the sheila over there will ya!'

butter wouldn't melt in his/her mouth
Someone who reeks of insincerity.

BUSIER THAN A ONE-ARMED TAXI DRIVER WITH THE CRABS

bye bye

Goodbye!

bye byes

What we do when we go to bed—we go to bye byes—pathetic isn't it. (See also *nye nyes*.)

B.Y.O.

Acronym for quaint Australian dining-out custom of 'Bringing Your Own' liquor to an unlicensed restaurant. It may also appear on a party invitation—bloody cheapskates!

CACTUS

cack

Anything a bit unpleasant or unsightly is said to be 'a bit cack'. Origin of word uncertain but nappies occasionally get filled with baby cack . . . so, figure it out for yourself!

cacked

A term used to describe something you do in your trousers when either terrified or highly amused. 'The bullet came so close to his head he almost cacked himself.' Or, 'He thought it was so funny, he almost cacked himself laughing.'

cackle berry

Simply an egg. Presumably the cackle comes from the sound made by the chicken when laying it. Which reminds me, what came first—the chicken or the egg? The chicken of course—can you imagine God sitting on an egg?

cactus

If something has become totally useless it is said to be 'cactus'. If a person contracts a terminal disease or suffers some sort of major misfortune, i.e. bankruptcy, loss of job etc.—they are also regarded as being cactus.

cakehole

Where you stick the bunghole—your mouth!

camp
> Homosexual male or female or some object or event associated with the homosexual community. I think my dog may be gay—I caught him listening to some Judy Garland records the other day!

camp as a row of Arab tents
> Term used to describe any flamboyant (generally male) homosexual who makes no secret of his proclivity. In fact he was sibilating so much, I thought it was escaping gas!

camp pie
> Compressed tinned meat—a bit like Spam and delicious in a white bread sandwich with tomato sauce!

cancer stick
> A cigarette—now available in packs of 50 so you can still fool yourself (and the doctor) that you're only on one pack a day!

Captain Cook
> The English discoverer of Australia back in 1788 who died after being speared in the Sandwiches (Islands that is). It's also rhyming slang for look. So now you know what we mean when we say we're taking a captains at something.

cardie
> Abbreviation for that fashion abomination—the cardigan—Perry Como and Andy Williams have got a lot to answer for!

cark
> To cark is simply to die. If your car breaks down to the point of no repair, it has carked it. In fact, it's totally cactus!

c'arn
> Abbreviation of phrase 'Come on!' Term used to encourage your team to victory, e.g. 'C'arn the mighty Lions' (famous Melbourne football team).

case
> Description for anyone a little eccentric. 'That bloke's a real case.' Or, for a real loser—'He's also a real hopeless case!'

Centre, the
> What we in Australia refer to as the middle of Australia—situated somewhere in

the Northern Territory and sometimes called either the Dead Heart (due to its isolation) or the Red Centre (due to the colour of the soil).

century, to knock up a
Generally alluding to hitting a hundred runs in cricket but can be applied to a hundred games of football, a hundred television shows or even celebrating your hundredth birthday. My grandfather never made it to his century . . . in fact he knew exactly the day he was going to die—the judge told him!

cert
Abbreviation of certainty—a dead cert at the racecourse is certainly worth putting the rent on.

chain, dragging the
Not pulling your weight, malingering.

chalkie
Nickname for a teacher. I remember my old geography teacher asking me what the capital of Alaska was. I told him 'A'!

charge like a wounded/Mallee bull, to
To charge an excessive fee for goods or services. (See also accountants, solicitors, plumbers, electricians etc.) Only gaggin' chaps!

CHEWIE ON YER BOOT

Charlie

Abbreviation of Charlie Wheeler—which is rhyming slang for sheila—meaning a member of the fairer sex. 'Let's go to the pub and check out the Charlies!'

cheerio (1)

In the Northern Territory and Queensland these are your small frankfurters or sausages. (See also **savs**, **little boys** and me in the locker room on a cold day!)

cheerio (2)

A friendly expression of farewell.

cheerio (3)

A greeting generally sent out over the radio. 'And it's a big cheerio to Bert and Gladys listening out there in Thomastown.' Talk about the cutting edge of controversial broadcasting!

cheese, the old

This term can be used to describe either your wife or mother. Shortened version of 'cheese and kisses' which is rhyming slang for missus.

cherry

Euphemism for a bright red, shiny new cricket ball. (And that thing you lose after your first sexual encounter . . . it took me about twenty tries!)

Chesty Bonds

Almost generic term for men's singlets originating from a 1930s cartoon character who had a magnificent physique and wavy blond hair. Still available at many menswear stores around Australia today.

chewie

Abbreviation of chewing gum.

chewie on yer boot!

A mild exclamation of derision used to put an opponent off his kick. Presumably, the chewie is designed to make his boot stick to the grass. Pretty radical huh?

chiack, to

Pronounced shy-ack, it means to jeer or scorn. 'The defeated players copped a chi-acking from their supporters as they left the field.'

DRY AS A CHIP

Chinaman, I must have killed a
Statement of absolutely no substance used to explain away a run of misfortune. So if everything's going 'wrong' for you, that could be the reason!

chinwag
Nothing your average Aussie likes better than hanging over the back fence and having a darn good chinwag (chat).

chip (1)
Aussie equivalent of the American French fry.

chip (2)
When you admonish somebody—you have just chipped them. 'George got chipped by the boss for arriving late for work again.'

chip, dry as a
To be very thirsty—dry as a chip of wood. Or description of drought conditions.

chip in, to (1)
To intercede in an argument or fight or to interrupt a conversation.

chip in, to (2)
Now, you remember George who got chipped by the boss for being late? Well, he did it once too often and now he's been given the 'Big A' so I'm passing the hat

around for everyone in the office to chip in to buy him a going-away present. (I could have saved a lot of space by simply saying 'to donate money'!)

chippie
What we call carpenters due to the fact they spend most of their day chipping away at bits of wood.

chock-a-block
An old sailor once told me this expression has something to do with a captain and a cabin boy but, in the interests of decency, it simply means completely full. A stadium, a train, a Christmas stocking can all be in this condition.

chockers
Simply an abbreviation of above.

chocko
Abbreviation of chocolate frog—rhyming slang for wog; these days an affectionate term for anyone of Mediterranean descent.

chocolate teapot, as useful as a
Obviously something useless—a bit like tits on a bull and the waterproof teabag!

CHOCKERS

choof off
What you do when you depart someone's company—as in a train leaving a station, you choof off.

chook
Aussie term for chicken, hen or rooster.

chookers
Show business expression of good luck bestowed on a performer just before he or she goes on stage—similar to 'break a leg'—another silly show-biz wish. My colleagues usually say, 'Have a heart attack!'

chooks, I hope your . . . turn into emus and kick your dunny down
Probably the most evil Aussie curse that can ever be wished upon someone. Fear not though, in our very short history this phenomenon has never eventuated.

chop, get in for your
Grab a share of what's rightfully yours.

chop, not much
If something or someone doesn't meet with your approval, it's not much chop.

chop, one . . . short of a barbeque
Mentally deficient—the light's on but nobody's home, keeps kangaroos in the top paddock, thinks the Supreme Court is where God plays tennis—get the picture!

chow shop

One great Aussie institution used to be going down to the local 'chow shop' (Chinese restaurant) with a large saucepan and bringing home enough sweet and sour to feed an army. We've got a Chinese/Jewish restaurant in our neighbourhood—it's called Sum Dum Goy!

Chrissie

Sorry, not an abbreviation of Christine but the ultimate slang obscenity for Christmas. People using it to describe dinner, gifts or holidays (in my humble but psychotic opinion) should be electrocuted!

Christmas, what else didja get for . . .?

Hard-hitting retort to any motorist sounding his horn to excess in traffic . . . it never quietens them down, but it can be a cathartic experience for you.

chrome dome

A follically challenged person. I'm losing hair so fast, my barber now charges a search fee!

chromies

Chrome wheels—of course!

chuck (1)

In Australia, we hardly ever throw something—we chuck it.

CHROME DOME

chuck (2)

Also in Australia, we hardly ever vomit or throw up—we chuck! (See also *chunder*.)

chucking a wobbly/spaz

Anyone who goes absolutely berserk with anger has just chucked a wobbly or spaz (as in convulsing like a spastic).

chunder

To throw up, puke, go for the technicolour yawn . . . how come there's always carrots?

ciggie

Very good! A cigarette.

clackers

Dentures. My old granddad left his in a glass beside the bed one night. He woke up the next morning to find them gone and replaced by a glassful of two cent pieces. (Tooth Fairy joke—for the humorously challenged.)

clanger, to drop a

Aussie equivalent of a faux pas.

clapped out

An exhausted car. Any vehicle barely running is clapped out. Indeed, performers in the twilight of their careers and not pulling the audiences they used to also fall into the clapped out category. But enough about me, let's move on to the next word shall we?

CHUNDER

clappers, to go like the
To move very fast. If your car isn't clapped out and has a powerful motor, it goes like the clappers.

Claytons
Brand-name of non-alcoholic beverage, the slogan for which was—'Claytons—the drink you have when you're not having a drink.' Claytons has now slipped into the Aussie vernacular to describe anything that resembles something it's not. Thus we can have a Clayton's marriage—where a man and woman live together pretending to be Mr and Mrs but sleeping in different beds—the marriage you have when you're not having a marriage—get it!

clip
A sharp slap generally delivered around the ears by your mum, dad or a policeman. 'His dad gave him a good clip under the ear for breaking the window.'

clobber (1)
To clobber someone is to strike them.

clobber (2)
Then there's the clobber you wear—clothes. A suit can be described as a nice set of clobber, cobber!

clocked
If you have just been clocked, you've just been clobbered. 'He got clocked on the nose.'

clout
Very similar to a clip—only your ears sting a bit longer!

club, in the pudding
Pregnant—and looking like a Christmas pudding!

clucky
Psychological condition that occurs in women (and some men) when they handle other people's babies—they are overcome by a strong desire to rush right home and make one of their own . . . gosh, I can feel another golf game coming on!

coathanger, the
So called because of its resemblance to one—the Sydney Harbour Bridge.

coat lifter
A male homosexual. (See also ***shirt lifter***.)

coat tailer/tugger
An annoying specimen generally found on a racecourse tugging at your coat for either money or a tip.

cobber
Anyone who is your friend is a cobber. It can also be used as a general expression like pal. 'G'day cobber, how's it all going?'

cock-and-bull
Any story that has a serious credibility gap is said to be a load of cock-and-bull.

cockatoo
As well as being a native Australian parrot, it is also the bloke who keeps watch for the police at an illegal gambling venue. Probably so named as domesticated cockatoos tend to screech warnings of impending visitations.

cock-up
The Aussie equivalent to the American screw-up—a terrible mistake—a total balls-up in fact!

cocky (1)
Abbreviation of cockatoo.

CODGER

cocky (2)
Abbreviation of cockroach (mainly Queensland).

cocky (3)
Self confident, arrogant—up yourself.

cocky (4)
Farmer or small-land owner. Depending on what he runs, he could be a cow cocky, fruit cocky, sheep cocky or a cane cocky. I suppose if he was a self confident farmer who raised cockatoos, he could be a cocky cocky cocky.

cocky's poop, not worth a pinch of
Something (or someone) totally worthless is said to have this attribute.

codger
An elderly gentleman.

cods
Euphemism for testicles. We suspect derived from male ballet dancer's cod piece.

codswallop
Absolute nonsense.

coffin nail
A cigarette—due probably to the fact that it's a dying habit. Yes folks, a reformed smoker here!

COLDER THAN A MOTHER-IN-LAW'S KISS

coit
Favourite Australian expression: 'A kick up the coit'. Your backside, bum, ring, dot, acre, arse, anus, freckle, Khyber etc. (See also **quoit**.)

colder than a mother-in-law's kiss
Pretty damn cold—so cold in fact, I saw a dog stuck to a fire hydrant!

cold enough to freeze the balls off a billiard table
And if you thought that was cold . . .

cold enough to freeze the walls off a bark humpy
Spoonerisitic corruption of 'cold enough to freeze the balls off a brass monkey'.

coldie
A blizzardly cold can of beer—you can't beat knocking back a couple of coldies in front of the old telly!

collected, to get
What happens when your opponent runs through you on the footy field or when you get run down by a car. My wife now has a glass bottom installed in her car so whenever she does run someone down she can see if it's anyone she knows!

Collins Street farmer
City dweller who owns a farm purely for tax relief as a primary producer. (See also *Pitt Street farmer*.)

collywobbles
Indefinable attack of nausea or upset stomach. Also, more recently referring to famous Victorian football team, Collingwood, who for many years tended to falter in performance just before important finals matches.

come at, I couldn't . . . that
Expression of rejection of a proposal of business, marriage, sex—oh all right, I'll give it one more try!

come off it!
Expression of disbelief or cynicism. John Blackman sexier than Richard Gere? 'Come off it!'

comic cuts
Rhyming slang for guts. 'He copped one right in the comics.'

compo
What every red-blooded Aussie yells out whenever he or she is injured at work. Abbreviation of Workers' Compensation where the government pays your salary while you recover.

conchie
Abbreviation for conscientious person. I spent most of my school days being un-conchie . . . or should that be unconscious!

conk
Yet another term for nose.

conk out, to
To expire, to die. Cars do it a lot and let's not even think about my libido!

connie
Generally, referring to both male and female tram and/or bus conductors. Due to government austerity measures, they are gradually becoming an endangered species in most states of Australia.

cooee
A loud bush call used to identify your location. If you are within cooee of something, you're very close. However, an oft used expression to indicate what a total miss would be. 'He didn't come within cooee of winning the tennis match.'

Coolgardie safe
Named after the rural West Australian town where it was invented. It's a hessian covered frame kept moist to preserve and keep cool perishable food-stuffs.

cop it, to
To receive a verbal or physical punishment. 'Boy, you're really gunna cop it from Mum and Dad for getting home so late last night.'

cop it sweet, to
It virtually means to take your punishment like a man—personally I'd prefer to take it like some other man.

copper (1)
A policeman, a walloper, the fuzz!

TO CRACK A TINNIE

copper (2)
A big laundry vat with a fire under it that your mother (or granny) used to boil clothes in prior to today's sophisticated washing machines and detergents.

copper (3)
A penny or farthing (no longer used as currency).

Cop Shop
Name of long-running Aussie television police series, another name for a police station.

cop-you-later
It means quite simply—see you again but, as is our want in Australia, it's nice to put some sexual connotation into everything we do—even a simple goodbye!

corker
If something's a real corker—it's great!

cornflakes packet, where did you get your licence, out of a
Angry response to motorists who drive badly.

cossie
Abbreviation of swimming costume.

cot case

You see them at pubs and parties drinking themselves into oblivion to the point where we put 'em in the cot to sleep it off. It can also relate to anyone mentally exhausted from the effects of stress brought on by six screaming kids.

cove

Another term for bloke. 'He's not a bad sort of cove.'

crack

Your anus (for the obvious reasons).

crack a fat, to

To have an erection.

crack a tinnie, to

Some blokes get more pleasure out of this than cracking a fat; to open a can of beer.

crackerjack

Adjective used to describe anything outstanding or someone with great talent. 'He's a crackerjack basketballer.'

cracker, to not have a

To be totally, utterly broke. (See also *razoo*.)

DOESN'T HAVE A CRACKER

crack hardy, to

To put on a brave front in the face of adversity. Personally, rather than crack hardy, I'd sooner crack a tinny!

crack on, to

Is what you do when trying to woo someone. There are many forms of cracking on to someone—it can involve buying her a drink, dinner, a car or just simply asking her, 'How about it love?'

crash hot

Something or someone of excellent quality. If you're not feeling well however, you are said to be not feeling too crash hot.

crawler

A sycophant. One might have to do a lot of crawling to the missus to be allowed to play golf more than twice a week.

cray

Abbreviation of crayfish (lobster).

creamed

If you cream the opposition, you have just annihilated them.

cricket

Rather complicated game invented by the Poms played with bat and hard, red leather ball. In Test matches, eleven players take the field along with two batsmen from the opposing side. At each end of the pitch (about 22 yards long and about eight feet wide) are three wooden sticks (the stumps) on top of which sit two little bits of wood (the bails). Ten players spread themselves around an oval-shaped playing field, one umpire positions himself behind the stumps at the end the bowler is to bowl from along with the non-striking batsman whilst the other umpire positions himself at right angles about 30 yards from the batsman on strike. The bowler rubs the ball on his groin area and runs in to bowl, it rains for five days and the match is declared a draw! Simple! Then of course, there are our limited over matches of 50 overs per side (over = six balls) which only take about seven hours to complete and are a tad more entertaining to watch.

crikey!

An expression of surprise—used especially when there's been a result in a Test match.

cripes!
> Similar expression of astonishment.

crook
> If you are feeling ill—you're a bit crook.

crook, to go . . . on
> If you go crook on someone, you have not just thrown up on them—you have severely admonished them. However, if you simply 'go crook'—you are merely complaining.

cross-country wrestling
> What Aussie rules fans unkindly term rugby league—probably due to the inordinate amount of manhandling required to complete a game.

crow-eater
> A resident of South Australia—their A.F.L. footy team is known as the Adelaide Crows.

crown jewels, the
> The complete set of the male genitalia. (See also *family jewels*.)

crows, stone the
> Another exclamation of surprise (originating in rural Australia and hardly ever used by a city slicker).

THE CUTS

cruel the pitch, to
To spoil someone's fun—sort of like maliciously digging up a cricket pitch.

crumpet, not worth a
Even though they're around $1.20 for a pack of six in our local supermarket, they can represent something totally worthless. Some say my writing has crumpet-like qualities!

cue, to put one's . . . on the rack
You've either retired, ceased fornicating or died. After over-imbibing, I'm capable of all three in one night!

cupid, my name's . . . not stupid
Something you say to someone to indicate you're not easily fooled. But then, if a fool and his money weren't easily parted—nobody would be doing any business.

cuppa
Abbreviation for 'cup of tea'. Favourite thing to do after some hard work or as a social activity. Let's sit down and have a cuppa—Australia's favourite panacea.

curry
To give someone 'a bit of curry' is to either angrily abuse them or to make them strive a little harder.

cut lunch, to throw a
Rhyming slang for 'to throw a punch'.

cuts, the
Now banned form of corporal punishment meted out (mainly on recalcitrant boys) at school. It involved the 'cuttee' putting both hands palm up in front of his body whilst a teacher would strike them with a leather strap. If you were particularly naughty, you'd get six strokes (six of the best).

I had a very strange headmaster—he gave me six of the best one day and then said, 'Now, you do it to me!' (See also *getting the strap*.)

DAG

Dad 'n' Dave

Two of the characters from Steele Rudd's book *On Our Selection*, a long-running radio serial and myriad dirty jokes involving Dave's girlfriend, Mabel. Also rhyming slang for shave.

dag

Anyone a little eccentric or amusing is regarded as a 'bit of a dag'.

daggy

Anything outdated, old fashioned or unattractive can be a bit daggy. E.g. beige leisure suit, white sox, grey shoes, green shirt and white belt would make you look very daggy.

dags (1)

Offensive substance hanging off a sheep's bottom.

Dags (2)

With profound apologies to any Dags reading this book (one in particular)—an abbreviation of the name Daryl.

daily double

If you've backed the winners of two designated races, you've won the Daily Double. It also applies to anything that happens in twos. E.g. if you marry a nymphomaniac who owns a pub—you've cracked it for the Daily Double! If she's a multimillionaire as well, congratulations—you've just landed the Trifecta!

daisy cutter
Term used in ball sports for any ball that skims just above the grass. (See also **worm-burner**.)

daks
Another term for trousers. When getting a penicillin injection, the doctor will invariably instruct you to 'drop your daks'.

Dame Nellie, doing a
Anyone who keeps retiring then returning does exactly this. As did our very own famous opera singer Dame Nellie Melba (1861–1931–32–33!). (A very sick mind at work here folks!)

damper
Rudimentary form of bush bread made from flour and water and cooked in the coals of a campfire.

Darwin stubbie
Exaggerated term for a two litre bottle of beer manufactured in the Northern Territory—presumably to slake their exaggerated thirsts due to the hot climate. (Normal size stubbie for us wimps down south is 375 ml—about 1/5th the size.)

date
No doubt due to its resemblance to one—your anus.

dated
One of the reasons an Aussie always smiles whenever they hear an American say their son or daughter has just started dating. Out here, if someone grabs you between the buttocks using their finger to excite your nether regions—you have just been dated and are well within your rights to turn around and smash them in the face—unless of course you enjoyed it! Most don't.

dead dingo's donger, drier than a
Pretty bloody thirsty! A dingo is a feral native dog found mainly in the Australian outback, a donger is something found hanging between your legs!

dead heart
The arid middle of the Northern Territory—so called because nothing much grows there. It's also what my barber calls the top of my scone!

dead horse
Rhyming slang for tomato sauce—particularly delicious on a dog's eye (pie).

dead horse, flogging a
Continuing a pointless argument or exercise.

dead marine
An empty beer bottle or can.

dead set
Spot on, fair dinkum, absolutely correct.

death adders in your pockets
Miser's measly excuse for not wanting to pay for anything. In fact, the last time he pulled his wallet out was because his pants were on fire!

decko, take a
Take a look.

deener
Term for pre-decimal shilling (now ten cents).

demo
Abbreviation of demonstration. You can stage a demonstration to protest against government policy or take a car you're about to purchase for a demo run.

DEATH ADDERS IN YOUR POCKETS

derro
A tramp or bum—abbreviation of derelict.

devo
Not only the name of a popular rock group but abbreviation for deviant.

dick, had the
Anything that has had the dick (or Richard) has just become totally useless.

dickhead
Description of a foolish person (generally male). A more polite expression can be Richard Cranium—also close relative of a wanker.

Dickless Tracy
Rather uncomplimentary (but quite descriptive) term for female police officer. I got pulled over by one for speeding. She said she'd let me off with a warning . . . fired two shots over my head!

diddle (1)
To diddle someone is to swindle them.

diddle (2)
To diddle yourself is to masturbate!

diff, what's the
Shortened version of 'what's the difference?'

dig, to have a
To have a dig at someone is to provoke them or be sarcastic towards them. If you've made an Aussie feel foolish he will often retort, 'Are you havin' a dig at me mate?'

digger
Originally a term for a nineteenth century Australian goldminer, it later became synonymous with the Australian foot soldier. 'G'day digger' is a very useful social tool when greeting someone whose name you've forgotten. (See also *shaggiedick*).

dill
An idiot or fool.

din-dins
Dare I say? Abbreviation of dinner.

ding

Expression used to describe a small dent in a car's bodywork. 'The car's OK except it's got a couple of dings here and there.'

dinger (1)

Euphemism for condom—you put it on your donger!

dinger (2)

Another term for your donger (or penis).

dinger (3)

Your anus—versatile little word ain't it?

dink (1)

When you give someone a ride on your bicycle, you are giving them a dink.

dink (2)

As you get older, dink becomes a euphemism for sexual intercourse—however there is no bike involved—unless the lady has a bit of a reputation in which case see *town bike*!

dinki-di

No, not the name of the town bike but expression used to describe anything or anyone of unquestionable quality or character. (See also *fair dinkum*.)

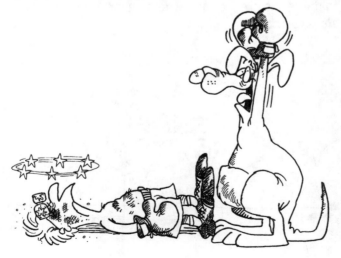

DONE LIKE A DINNER

dinner, done like a
Thoroughly and utterly defeated.

dip (1)
Not only something you do when dancing but also term for a pick-pocket.

dip (2)
Description of someone a little eccentric—shortened version of 'dip-shit'.

dip, to have a
To attempt something or get involved in a fight. It is therefore possible to 'have a dip at having a dip!'

dip out on, to
To miss out on an opportunity or to not show up for an appointment. 'Joe was to meet us at the game, but he dipped out on us.'

dirty, to be a bit . . . on
To be a bit cross with someone.

dirty, to do the . . . on
That's why you're a bit dirty on someone—they've just betrayed a trust.

dishlickers
One of the many terms greyhound owners never use to describe their pooches. (See also **rats on sticks**.)

DISHLICKERS

divvy
Abbreviation for dividend—'Stand by for tote divvies, punters'. Or, what you do when equally apportioning something—'Let's divvy up the winnings between us'. Or, that lump of turf dislodged whilst playing golf (divot).

divvy van
Something your wife never likes to see you arrive home in the back of—a police divisional wagon.

do (1)
A party. 'Harry's putting on a bit of a do on Saturday night.'

do (2)
So I guess Gladys will be off to the hair salon for a do (hair-do) so she'll look her best for it!

dob (1)
The very un-Australian act of tattle-tailing on someone. 'George dobbed in his mate for taking a sickie—what a dobber!'

dob (2)
Generally used to describe the kicking of a goal—'He's dobbed it right through the middle!'

doco
Abbreviation of documentary.

dog, head like a robber's
Used generally to describe a very ugly female. So ugly, she's got a job standing outside pharmacies making people sick!

dog's balls, to stick out like
Anything that's blatantly obvious sticks out like dog's balls. My dog doesn't have his any more—he just sits there in the corner—glaring at me every day!

dog's eye
Rhyming slang for that great Aussie gastronomic institution—the meat pie. Delicious with a dob of dead horse (tomato sauce) on the top.

dole bludger
Any person who is capable of work but chooses not to and lives off social welfare payments.

Don, the
Affectionate title of one of Australia's finest cricketers during the 30s and 40s—Sir Donald Bradman.

dong (1)
Something you do when you hit somebody—you dong them.

dong (2)
Yet another euphemism for the penis.

donger
Yet another euphemism for the previous euphemism!

donk (1)
Yet another euphemism for the previous two euphemisms!

donk (2)
A car engine. You can't beat a car with a good donk under the bonnet.

donkey, why don't you turn into a . . . and get onto yourself!
Mild expletive used to tell someone to wise up to themselves.

do over
To beat the living crap out of someone. 'Poor old Nick got done over by a gang of hoods last night.'

WHY DON'T YOU TURN INTO A DONKEY
AND GET ON TO YOURSELF!

dose, to cop a (1)

To contract a venereal disease.

dose, to cop a (2)

To be roundly criticised . . . so, it is possible to cop a dose from your boss without actually sleeping with him!

dose of salts, to go through like a

Referring to the laxative qualities of this substance, it means to be thoroughly trounced.

dosh

Cash!

dot

Your anus. Favourite Aussie pastime—sitting on your dot doin' nuthin'.

Down Under

If a bloke comes up to you and tells you he's very big Down Under girls, don't slap his face. He's actually telling you he's a very important Aussie! Down Under is what the rest of the world calls Australia.

dragged, to be

It's what the coach does to a football player if he doesn't follow orders or is playing below standard—he gets dragged from the field.

DRIER THAN A POMMY'S BATH TOWEL!

draining the dragon

Urinating. (See also **syphon the python**, **looking down on the unemployed**, **shaking hands with the wife's best friend**, **splashing the boots** and **taking a slash**.)

drier than a Pommy's bath towel

Very thirsty and a rather unkind suggestion that our friends from Mother England aren't too fond of bathing.

drip

Close relation of the dill, drongo and nerd. Dill, Drongo & Nerd—also the name of my accountancy firm!

drongo

The name of a Victorian racehorse from the early 20s who always finished at or near the tail of the field. No-hopers now take the title.

droob

Slow, pathetic person. Close relation to drip, drongo and nerd.

drop

To drop someone is to knock them to the ground with a punch.

drop a bucket

To surprise a rival with hitherto unknown embarrassing facts.

DROP

PSST! PSST! !

DROP A BUCKET

dropping your bundle

To lose control of a situation resulting in complete and utter confusion.

drover's dog

Someone of little or no importance . . . however the dog would probably dispute that!

dubbo

A person of limited mental capacity—but definitely *not* a reflection on the population of the rural New South Wales town of the same name!

duck

In the game of cricket, a batsman who gets dismissed without scoring a run has scored a duck. So, when you hear of a batsman going out for a duck, he is not a poultry fancier!

duckhouse, that's one up against your

Meaningless jibe indicating minor victory in trivial dispute.

ducks and drakes (1)

Rhyming slang for the delirium tremens—the shakes.

ducks and drakes (2)

If someone's playing ducks and drakes with you, they're giving you the old runaround.

duck's disease

If you are vertically challenged you are suffering duck's disease—in other words, your bum is too close to the ground. I'm not short—if you don't believe me, give us a ring and my wife will hold me up to the phone!

duck shove

To move an issue around in ever diminishing circles until it ceases to become your responsibility and disappears up its fundamental orifice.

duck, wet enough to bog a

Now that's incredibly wet and rainy!

duds

Another name for clothing—in particular trousers. (See also *daks*.)

duffer (1)

Australian equivalent of a cattle rustler.

duffer (2)

A worthless gold mine.

WET ENOUGH TO BOG A DUCK

duffer, a silly

Term used to describe someone who has done something a little foolish or has had a minor mishap. 'Oh you silly duffer, you've just broken my best vase!'

dummy

What Americans call a baby pacifier. My mother used a baseball bat on me!

dummy bid

Real estate term for bid taken from an imaginary bidder by the auctioneer at house auctions. A dummy bidder is generally disguised as a letterbox or a tree!

dummy, to spit the

To throw a tantrum or get very irate. Relating to baby spitting out dummy and crying loudly. (See also ***chuck the Glo-mesh into the shagpile***.)

dunny

Outdoor toilet generally located at the 'bottom' of your garden. These days used as general term for any toilet.

dunny man

The guy with the unenviable job of collecting the by-products of the dunny. Sometimes called the nightman (he came at night to perform this unpleasant task) or the pan man (he used to hoist the pan on his head) and place it on his lorry (dunny truck). If you are feeling depressed, you are said to be 'Flatter than a shit carter's hat!'

DUMMY BID

durry
> A cigarette or cigarette butt.

dyke (1)
> Euphemism for dunny.

dyke (2)
> Lesbian.

dykes in spikes
> Lesbian golfers.

DUNNY

EARBASHER

earbasher
An incessant talker . . . I haven't spoken to my wife for ten years—I don't like to interrupt her!

early opener
Any hotel that opens at around 6 a.m. to cater for shift workers or drunks who have just been thrown out of a pub that *closes* at 6 am.

eau de cologne
Rhyming slang for telephone.

eighteen
An eighteen gallon keg of beer generally found in a pub's cellar but occasionally found at a serious party or barbeque. If you only need enough to keep you and your mate going for a couple of hours—order a niner.

elbow grease
That non-existent, indefinable substance that your mum, dad, wife, husband or boss tells you to use when they want you to put a bit more effort into a chore. 'C'mon, use a bit of elbow grease will ya!'

ekka, the
Located in Queensland, the Brisbane Exhibition Grounds (ekka—short for exhibition of course). Also abbreviation of the name Eric.

ELBOW GREASE

elephants
Abbreviation of elephant's trunk—rhyming slang for drunk. So drunk—all he remembers is giving the cop a specimen—in his gun holster!

emma chisit
No, not a famous suffragette. It's simply a very strine (Australian) way of asking, 'How much is it?'

emu
A character who wanders around the betting ring looking for discarded betting tickets in the faint hope one will be a winner.

emu parade
School or military parade formed for the express purpose of picking up litter.

end, getting your . . . in
Managing to achieve some sort of sexual intercourse.

en-zed
Abbreviation for country across the Tasman—New Zealand. Ideal opportunity to do tacky joke about New Zealanders and their close relationship with sheep but, in the interests of selling this book in the land of the long white cloud—shall resist the temptation!

ELEPHANTS

esky

Now almost generic trademarked term for portable icebox (I think I married one) or car fridge. Often found at football or cricket matches and ideal for standing on if you are vertically challenged. We suggest you do not try standing on the poly-styrene model—you could finish up structurally challenged!

ESKY

euchred

Exhausted, worn-out, useless, totally stuffed (or rooted!). You could be totally euchred after spending a couple of hours push-starting a euchred car.

ex

Your ex-wife, ex-husband, ex-mother-in-law—your ex-bank account.

EUCHRED AFTER GETTING YOUR END IN

FANG

face fungus
> Any hairy facial growth. 'Is that a beard or are you eating a dog?' 'Is that a moustache or just your eyebrows coming down for a drink?'

fag
> Euphemism for bloke who prefers the company of another bloke. Also another term for a cigarette. Hence, it is possible to bum a fag from a fag!

fair crack of the whip
> Exclamation demanding fair play.

fair dinkum
> If anyone or anything is fair dinkum you bet your life it's totally genuine. Fair dinkum!

fair enough
> General expression indicating accord or agreement—OK? Fair enough!

fair suck of the sauce bottle
> See also *fair crack of the whip*.

fair suck of the sav

Sav is short for saveloy—a small savoury sausage. Same meaning as the whip and the sauce bottle!

family jewels, the

The penis and testicles. (See also *crown jewels*.)

fang

To borrow some money is to fang. Remember that old adage though—'Neither a fanger nor a fangee be'. Geez, I wish I'd said that!

fanging it

Driving your car at high speed . . . I only speed because I figure the less time I spend on the road, the less chance I have of having a prang!

Farmer Giles

Rhyming slang for piles or haemorrhoids.

fat as a match

Someone of very thin build—whenever he gets his front sunburnt, his back peels!

FAT AS A MATCH

father's day, happy as a bastard on
Obviously not a happy chappie. I had a rather unhappy childhood—I got home from school one day and my parents had shifted!

fat, to chew the
To have a chat.

fat, to crack a
To have an erection—hopefully, not in the middle of chewing the fat!

fattie
Slang term for $1,000.

fatties
Very wide car tyres.

fence, a bit over the
An unreasonable proposition or fee is said to be a bit over the fence.

fencing wire, as tough as
A bit like my wife when I ask her if I can play golf for a third time this week!

ferret, giving the . . . a run
Having sexual intercourse.

fess up, to
To confess.

fibber
Mild lie teller who tells fibs.

fibro
A substance that nearly every holiday home used to be made from due to its cheapness. Short for fibro-cement sheeting—impervious to almost everything except cricket balls!

fit as a Mallee bull
I've never seen a Mallee bull in a gym, but it means to be feeling on top of the world—if you're feeling even better than this, you are 'fit as a Mallee bull, and twice as dangerous!'

FIVE FINGER DISCOUNT

five finger discount
Shoplifting and/or stealing.

fiz-gig
Originally a police informer but nowadays a term used when you can't remember somebody's name. 'I saw old fiz-gig from school at the cricket the other day.'

flake (1)
Something you do after too much to drink—you flake (as in flake out). It can also mean to stay overnight at a friend's. 'I went over to Jack's place to flake for the night.'

flake (2)
What we Aussies call the flesh of the shark. Traditional Friday night meal—flake and chips (fries) with plenty of salt, vinegar or even tomato sauce!

flaming
Adjective used to describe or accentuate an event or person. 'He's a flaming good bloke who runs a flaming good pub with a flaming good dance band.'

flat chat
At full speed—flat chat in my car is about 60 kilometres an hour!

flat out, like a lizard drinking
Working very feverishly.

flatter than a shit carter's hat
Depressed. (See *dunny man*.)

flatties
Women's low-heeled shoes.

flick, the
To throw away or reject something is to give it the flick. Therefore, you may give an old, useless car the flick, breaking off an engagement is giving him or her the flick or just simply cutting someone short is also giving them the flick. I'm about to give this word the flick and move on to the next one.

flicks
Going to the flicks in Oz means going to the cinema. The word flicks originated from the early days when the movie would flicker on to the screen. The last movie I went to there was violence, torrid sex and a couple of thrilling chases. Then the film started and everyone settled down!

flies, drinking with the
Drinking alone. Being unsociable.

TO FLAKE OUT

DRINKING WITH THE FLIES

flies, no . . . on him
Expression of admiration indicating that a person is extremely astute and not easily duped. Oft quoted expression describing someone who has learned from being previously duped is, 'There's no flies on him—but you can see where they've been'.

flipping
Used in place of that other infamous 'F' word to express disgust or contempt. 'Why don't you flipping well go to hell!'

floater
A South Australian gastronomic monstrosity (but not to them) of a meat pie floating in a bowl of pea soup. Adelaide—indigestion city!

flog, to (1)
To steal.

flog, to (2)
To sell. Joe's got a job flogging brain operations door-to-door!

flog, to (3)
To unmercifully trounce. 'Our team copped a thorough flogging—250 to nil!'

flogger

A huge bunch of streamers (in your team's colours) and attached to the end of a stick. You 'flog' it up and down whenever they score a goal or to distract the opposition when they're lining up for one.

flogging the log

Masturbating.

fluff, to (1)

A small mistake. 'Jane made a bit of a fluff in her calculations.'

fluff, to (2)

To break wind—minor version of fart.

fluke

A lucky break. 'That hole in one was a real fluke.'

flying fox

Not only one of those stupid contraptions it was always mandatory to erect whilst attending boy scout camps, but also rhyming slang for the pox (venereal disease).

AFTER DRINKING A FOURPENNY DARK

Flynn, in like
Allegedly alluding to the social prowess of legendary Aussie film actor, Errol Flynn. To be successful in seducing a woman.

footie (1)
Abbreviation of football. (The 'T' should always be sounded as a 'D' in Ozspeak!)

footie (2)
In Australia, you're never going to a football game—you're 'garna footie'.

form, how's your rotten
Admonishment directed at someone who has just had some good luck but didn't include you in their good fortune.

fourpenny dark
Really cheap red wine originally served in a miniature mug with a slogan that went: 'Around the world for fourpence!' (About five cents.) I can get about half-way round with a bottle of really cheap vodka!

franger
A condom. With apologies to one of the world's great golfers, rhyming slang these days would have your dad saying before a hot date, 'Don't forget your Bernhard Langers!'

freckle
Your anus.

freckle puncher
Male homosexual—please don't ask me to go into gory details, just use your imagination!

Freddie, blind
Mythical person used to accentuate the blatantly obvious. 'Even blind Freddie could've told you that your marriage wouldn't last!'

Fred Nerk
Aussie equivalent of John Doe, Joe Blow or any other Tom, Dick or Harry.

free, a
A penalty kick awarded in Aussie Rules football. Also, when someone has let down their guard and admitted a mistake and allows you to roundly criticise them, they have just awarded *you* a free kick.

freight
> Money.

Fremantle doctor
> This doc doesn't make house-calls nor can you claim him on Medicare. It's actually the cooling afternoon breeze that seems to blow into Fremantle and Perth each afternoon.

French letter
> Yet another euphemism for a condom. My birth certificate is a letter of apology from the Acme French Letter Co!

Frenchy
> Yet another term for our little rubber chums!

frog and toad
> Rhyming slang for road.

front
> Bold, brash or cheeky. If you have all three of these attributes, you have 'more front than Myer/Grace Bros' (large Melbourne and Sydney department stores with huge street frontages).

front up, to
> Basically, it simply means to show up for an appointment . . . to make an appearance.

FULLER THAN A SEASIDE DUNNY
ON BOXING DAY

froth, couldn't blow the . . . off a beer
Pathetically weak or out of breath.

fuck truck
Generally speaking, any young bloke who gets around in a panel van (and he's not a plumber or carpenter) is accused of owning this vehicle for only one reason—he's too mean to pay for a cheap, sleazy motel somewhere. Get the picture? (See also *shaggin' wagon*.)

full
Drunk. 'Harry got home full at way past midnight.'

full as a boot
Very drunk.

full as a goog
Same drunk—or you could be full of food.

fuller than a Catholic state school
Again, in an intoxicated state. Non-private Catholic primary schools used to have very large classes.

fuller than a seaside dunny on Boxing Day
As it's always hot at Christmas in Australia, it's almost a tradition that the whole family goes to the beach on Boxing Day . . . again, yet another phrase alluding to intoxication!

fun bags
A woman's breasts. Sorry girls, I just write the definitions.

fungus features
Any bloke (or woman!) with a beard.

funny farm
Mental hospital. (See also *looney bin*.)

fuzzy wuzzy angels
Military jargon for frizzy-haired native stretcher-bearers of New Guinea during World War Two.

'G', the
Affectionate term for one of the world's most magnificent sporting arenas that can hold up to 100,000 spectators—the Melbourne Cricket Ground or M.C.G. (Not hard to tell I'm a proud Melburnian eh!)

Gabba, the
Affectionate term for one of the world's most magnificent sporting arenas that can hold up to 40,000 spectators (well I would like this book to sell well *all* over Australia)—the Queensland Cricket Association oval. Called the Gabba due to its location in the suburb of Woollongabba.

gab, gift of the
Anyone who has no trouble talking about any subject at any time has this dubious quality. My mother-in-law almost drowned at the beach—the lifesaver was trying to give her mouth-to-mouth but she wouldn't stop talking!

ga-ga
Mad or insane. Also, if you are deeply in love with someone, you are ga-ga over them.

g and c
Graft and corruption.

GA-GA

galah
Loud, rude, badly behaved person. Also an Australian parrot.

galah session
No doubt due to the galah's propensity for making a lot of noise. A galah session is also a gossip session on the outback radio network of the Royal Flying Doctor Service.

galoot
An idiot—very close relation of drip, drongo, droob and nerd.

game as Ned Kelly
As was the infamous Australian bushranger, anyone who is foolhardy, adventurous and fearless.

game as a pissant
Very courageous but then, you can be 'as drunk as a pissant' (which is probably why you're being so brave!). Crikey this is a confusing language!

gander, taking a
Taking a look at something. 'Take a gander at this will ya!'

garbo
Trash collector. They prefer to be known as garbologists—it looks so much better on their CVs.

gasbag
Someone full of wind who is an incessant talker. Aussie equivalent of American windbag.

gay and hearty
Rhyming slang for party.

gazunder
For sufferers of nocturnal incontinence—the humble chamber pot that 'goes under' the bed ready for any emergency.

g'day
Probably the most famous of all Australian phrases (thanks to Paul Hogan). It is our way of saying 'Hi there', although some tourists seem to think it can be a term of farewell—wrong!

geebung

Generic term describing a remote town or crass native-born Australian from A.B. Patterson's poem: 'It was somewhere up the country, in a land of rock and scrub, that they formed an institution called the Geebung Polo Club.' A geebung is also a native plum—variously described as a small and tasteless fruit—boy, have I worked with a few of *those* in radio and television over the years!

gee gees, the

The racecourse (of course!).

geek, take a

Take a look. If you're leafing through this dictionary in a bookstore, you're taking a geek.

gerry (1)

Abbreviation of geriatric. Grandpa is getting so old, his back goes out more often than he does!

Gerry (2)

Slang term for a German (or 'Jerry').

gerry (3)

That pot that goes under the bed each night. (See also *jerry*.)

GERRY

get off yourself
Stop talking or boasting about yourself.

ghost, grey
Victorian parking officer who, dressed in grey, can seemingly materialise as an apparition from nowhere to book unsuspecting illegally parked cars.

gig
Strange, odd or eccentric person.

gig, take a
Same as taking a geek—taking a look.

giggle house
Mental asylum. (Some would say, see also *Parliament House*!)

ging
Rudimentary type of slingshot made from thin strip of rubber inner tube.

ginger (1)
Your anus.

ginger (2)
Horse manure—due no doubt to its colour.

ginger (3)
To goad or urge someone to perform better is to give them a bit of ginger.

Ginger Meggs
Eternally youthful comic strip character whose exploits typify the average Australian pre-teens school boy. Arch enemy—Tiger Kelly, perennial girlfriend—Minnie.

giveaway, dead
Obvious clue. This dictionary is a dead giveaway that as an author I make a great shoe salesman!

give, to . . . it away
To abandon a task or quest. 'Bert was studying to be a rocket scientist but decided to give it away.'

glass door, as useful as a . . . on a dunny
An understatement to say something or someone has become fairly useless.

AS USEFUL AS A GLASS DOOR
ON A DONNY

Glomesh, chuck the . . . into the shagpile
To lose one's temper and storm out. (See also ***dummy, to spit the***.)

glory box
Aussie girls' equivalent of the American hope chest. Container used by prospective brides for toasters, vertical grills, cookbooks, antidotes etc.

gnat's nasty, missed by a
Missed by the barest of margins—a gnat's nasty is slightly smaller than a bee's dick. (See also ***poofteenth***.)

goanna (1)
Large Australian lizard.

goanna (2)
Rhyming slang for large Australian piano (peeanna!).

goat, ran like a hairy
Term used to describe a racehorse that didn't run as well as it could have.

Godzone
Strine term for Australia—'God's own' country!

goer
Anything that looks like being successful is classed as a goer in Australia.

Other variations include a female who is free with her favours or a very talented sportsperson.

going the knuckle
To punch someone (with a knuckle sandwich!).

golly
What you say whenever you discover one on your face—a pimple!

gone for a ride on the padre's bike
Barely believable alibi to cover somebody's whereabouts.

gone to Gowings
Originally advertising slogan to explain deserted streets—they've gone to Gowings for the bargains. Gowings—a Sydney retailer.

gong
An award bestowed upon one by either the Queen or the Australian government. I have been gonged several times—not for services to the community . . . just for not remembering the odd wedding anniversary or three!

gong, had the
Anything that outlived its usefulness or has expired has had the gong. (See also *had the sword*.)

GONE FOR A RIDE ON THE PADRE'S BIKE

Gong, the (1)
Abbreviation for the New South Wales city of Wollongong.

Gong, the (2)
Affectionate nickname of Yvonne Cawley who, as Yvonne Goolagong, became the first ever Aboriginal to win the Wimbledon singles tennis title.

good nick
If something is in good nick, it's in good condition. If you're in good nick, you're feeling (and looking) great!

good-oh
Aussie equivalent of OK. 'See you tomorrow.' 'Yeah, good-oh!'

good on ya!
Well done mate!

good, to come
This can either mean to recover from an illness or to deliver the goods. 'I thought Harry was going to leave without paying but he's come good with a cheque.'

go off, to (1)
To be free with one's sexual favours. If a female 'goes off', she is much sought after.

go off, to (2)
To putrefy. 'This butter's gone off—we'd better throw it out.' (See also *turf it.*)

go off, to (3)
To be stolen. 'My car went off last night.'

googie egg
What we call an egg to make it seem more appetising to a child (or husband!)

gooley (1)
A small stone or pebble used for throwing.

gooley (2)
An unspeakable secretion that dangles from a nostril when you don't blow your nose properly. (I think I'm going to throw up!)

GOOSE

goom
 Aboriginal term for methylated spirits.

goose (1)
 A foolish person.

goose (2)
 When you sneak up behind someone and grab them between the buttocks, you have just goosed (or dated) them. Be sure it's always someone you know and that they might actually enjoy this unique Australian form of greeting . . . otherwise you could finish up in a casualty ward or court!

goose's neck
 Rhyming slang for cheque. (See also *Gregory Peck*.)

Gordon, in more trouble than Speed
 Comic strip character always in dire straits. (U.S.—*Flash Gordon*.)

gorilla
 Another term for $1,000. (See also *fattie*.)

grafter
 Someone who toils away at his/her job.

graft, to . . . out a living
Working very hard to barely make ends meet.

grand piano, couldn't find a . . . in a one-roomed house
Let's face it, anyone this stupid has the IQ of a rubber plant!

Granny Smiths
God didn't make little green apples—Maria Ann Smith did (until she died in 1870). Granddad's on a special apple diet—he eats all the Granny Smiths he likes—except Grandma hides his dentures!

grape on the business, a
A spoilsport.

grass castles
Modern day term for mansions built from the proceeds of the sale of the wacky-tobbacky, marijuana. Personally, I think reality is a crutch for people who can't handle pot!

greaser
A despicable sycophant—close relation of the crawler.

GRASS CASTLES

GREASER

greasy pig

In that great Aussie gambling pastime, two-up, finally throwing tails after a succession of heads.

Great White Shark

Fairly prevalent around our beaches and of course, the nickname of Australian golfing legend, Greg Norman. Greg and I have a lot in common—we're both Aussies, we've both got blond hair and we both own a set of golf clubs!

greenie

An environmentalist—generally found chained to trees in rainforests singing 'We shall overcome'.

Gregory Peck

Rhyming slang for cheque. My bank manager rang to tell me I was overdrawn. I yelled at him, 'Do I ring you when you've too much of *my* money!'

grizzle

Complain, whine, whinge.

grizzleguts

A complaining, whining whinger!

grog

Booze, alcohol.

grog shop
Bottle shop (generally attached to a hotel).

grot (1)
A person of dirty thoughts and habits.

grot (2)
Pornographic movies. They can lead to violence—particularly when your wife comes home unexpectedly and finds you watching them with your mates!

grouse
Excellent. You can drive a grouse car, live in a grouse house with a grouse job and get to go out with some grouse sheilas! What a grouse life!

grouter, to come in on the
To take advantage of somebody else's efforts. A bit like taking home the girl your mate's been chatting up all night.

Grout, your Wally
If an Aussie says that to you in a pub, it's your turn to buy a round of drinks. 'It's your Wally Grout' is rhyming slang for 'it's your shout' (Wally Grout—noted Australian wicket-keeper). Also rhyming slang for stout and snout.

grub
Yet another person of unclean thoughts and habits.

guernsey, to get a
To win a place on a football team (or any team for that matter) or be accepted for a job.

gummies
Slang for gumboots, long rubber boots generally worn by farmers or me washing the car.

gum-sucker
A native of the state of Victoria (gum as in gum tree).

gumtree, happy as a possum up a
Although I've never asked one, I believe they are blissfully happy and contented.

HAPPY AS A POSSUM UP A GUMTREE

gumtree, up a
Well the possum may be happy but, if you're a human up a gumtree, figuratively speaking you are stranded or stymied.

gun
A top class sheep shearer.

gunner
Someone who procrastinates—always gunner do this and gunner do that. The sort of person who used to be indecisive but now they're not so sure!

gunner, rear
Male homosexual (who's probably never been anywhere near a Lancaster bomber!).

gurgler, down the
When something fails, it is said to have gone down the gurgler (plughole).

gutser, to come a
To come a gutser is to either fall over or fail at some endeavour.

guts, in the
As the phrase suggests, it means right in the middle. A football kicked right through the middle of the goal posts is regarded as through the guts.

guts, rough as
> Description of an ugly person or how you're feeling the next morning after a big party. (You probably look as rough as guts also!)

guts, spilling your
> No, not throwing up but 'fessing up. Telling everything you know to either the cops or a close friend.

gutter gripper
> Dickheads who drive along with their arm out of the window gripping the roof gutter.

gymp
> Anyone who walks with a limp is a gymp (with a gympy leg).

gyp, to
> To swindle (pronounced jip).

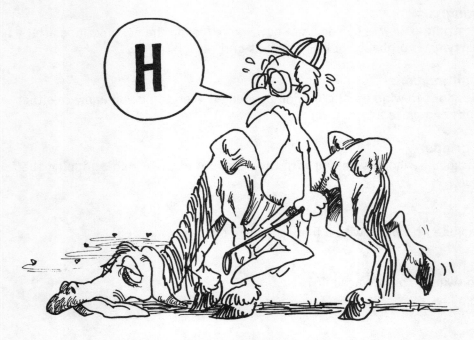

COULDN'T HEAD A DUCK

hair, grown too tall for his
Going bald—I have thin hair, but then again, who wants fat hair!

halfback flanker
Rhyming slang for wanker. (See also *merchant banker*.)

hammer, to be on someone's
To pressure someone from behind in a race or to constantly nag.

handbag
Male companion a lady takes to a social function when she's 'between companions'. Generally speaking, his job is merely to give her friends the impression that she can still attract a bloke!

happy as Larry
Blissfully contented.

happy as a pig in muck/shit
As blissfully contented as Larry!

harbour city, the
The beautiful harbour-surrounded city of Sydney—site of the 2000 Olympics. (See also **steak and kidney**.)

hard word, putting the . . . on
This can mean either asking a man or woman for a sexual favour or (if that fails) to lend you some money so you can go out and pay for a sexual favour.

hatful, ugly as a . . . of arseholes
Not that anyone has ever seen a hatful of these, but pretty damn ugly I would imagine!

have on, to
To deceive or dupe.

head a duck, couldn't
Racing jargon for an inferior racehorse.

heading 'em
Tossing two 'heads' in a game of two-up.

head like a twisted sandshoe
Incredibly ugly.

SCARCE AS HENS' TEETH

head, pull your . . . in
  Retort specifically designed to tell someone to shut up or not to interfere.

heads, I've seen better . . . on a beer
  Description of an unpleasant countenance.

heads, I've seen better . . . on a boil
  Just a tad uglier.

hens' teeth, scarce as
  Extremely rare. Well, have you ever seen a chook with choppers?

herbs, giving it some
  Tramping on the accelerator of a car to see what she'll do.

hey diddle diddle
  Rhyming slang for piddle (urinate).

hide the sausage/weenie/banana
  Euphemism for sexual intercourse. (See also **sink the sav**.)

highway robbery
  Any exorbitant fee charged for goods or services.

HIGHWAY ROBBERY

hip pocket in a singlet, as useful as a
About as useful as a chocolate teapot or a waterproof teabag!

hip pocket nerve
Located adjacent to your buttocks and where one keeps one's wallet. It tends to jump with every price or tax hike.

holding, how ya . . .?
An enquiry as to your current financial state. Generally followed up by a request to borrow a small amount. Can also be used to cadge a cigarette.

hollow log, going for a
Rhyming slang for going for a bog (to defecate).

home and hosed
Racing parlance for a racehorse that wins so easily as to be home and in its stable being hosed down while the others are still running.

home with a rug on
No, not sitting around the house wearing a wig! It virtually means the same as home and hosed.

homing pigeons, couldn't lead a flock of
Description of incompetent leadership—oft applied to politicians.

HOONING

I'M SO HUNGRY I COULD EAT A HORSE....
AND CHASE THE JOCKEY

hooks, to put the . . . into
To borrow money. 'He hooked him for $20.'

hoon
A larrikin with a propensity for showing off. Driving around in a brightly coloured car with a very loud exhaust is called hooning around.

hoop
A jockey—so called because of the coloured rings on their silks.

horse, I'm so hungry I could eat a . . . and chase the jockey
Pretty damn hungry!

horse's hoof
Rhyming slang for poof (male homosexual). Can be shortened to 'horse's'. Another oft used expression is 'cow's hoof'.

hospital pass
In football, one of those passes from your team mate that puts you at immediate physical peril from the opposition. So much so, that soon after receiving the ball, you go straight to hospital!

HOSPITAL PASS

hostie
Abbreviation of air hostess. These days, with the introduction of chaps into the profession they prefer to be called flight attendants.

hotter than a shearer's armpit
Not that anyone's ever stuck their nose up there and survived—but pretty darn hot!

hottie
Abbreviation of hot water bottle.

house on fire, to get on like a
To find someone else's company very pleasing.

howzat?
Loud exclamation made by bowler to umpire in game of cricket to ascertain if a batsman is out or not. Another expression sometimes used is 'Howizzie!'

hubbie
Wot else?! Abbreviation for husband.

Hughie
God. His immenseness. Drought stricken farmers will often incant 'Send her down Hughie!'

HOSTIE

hum

Anything on the nose or a bit smelly is said to have a bit of a hum about it.

hump, to

Well, in the USA it means to fornicate but, here in Australia mate, it means to carry. Swagmen hump their bluey, you may hump wood in from the shed and, indeed, if your wife is having trouble walking up a steep path, it's permissible to hump her—even in mixed company!

humpy

A mean, rudimentary bush dwelling generally made from corrugated iron and hessian.

HOWZAT

COLOURFUL RACING IDENTITY

icebergs
>   Men and women of seemingly diminished mentality who go swimming in the ocean in the dead of winter—in fact, I know a Goldberg who's an iceberg!

ice drill
>   Very similar activity to the above but performed very early in the chill of morning in shorts and generally by members of the armed forces.

ice-oh
>   Relative of the rabbit-oh and the bottle-oh—back in the days of ice-chests, the man who brought the ice. My old man used to think I was the dead spit of our ice-oh . . . hmmm!

identity, colourful racing
>   Euphemism for racetrack frequenter of dubious, untrustworthy character.

idiot box
>   The television!

IDIOT BOX

idiot sheets
Cardboard prompt cards used by some of us idiots who work in television and can't remember our lines.

iffy
Anything 'a bit iffy' is suspect or risky with unreliable origins—best not to get involved.

illywhacker
A confidence man who used to operate around country shows and fairs. Now, we just elect them into parliament!

IFFY

I'm-all-right-jackness
Not giving a tinker's cuss about your fellow human beings.

improve, on the
Generally alluding to someone recuperating in hospital.

innings
Length of time spent batting in the game of cricket or, if you die at 70 plus, every-one at your funeral will agree that you had a 'pretty good innings'.

Irish
Abbreviation for wig—derived from rhyming slang, Irish jig. Oh that *is* a wig—for a moment I thought you were wearing a drugged koala on your head!

iron lung, wouldn't work in an
Someone so lazy, they wouldn't even breathe without help.

ironed out, to be
To be knocked senseless or to drink until you pass out. 'Jack really ironed himself out last night and, when he got home, his missus ironed him out!'

irrits
Giving someone the irrits is to really annoy (or irritate) them.

IRRITS

Ities

Pronounced: eye-tyes. Abbreviation from World War Two vernacular for Italians. Even today, some Aussies from that era refer to them as 'Eye-talians'.

ivories

The teeth.

ivories, to tickle the

To play the goanna—the piano.

IVORIES

JACKAROO

jack/jacksie
Your backside, buttocks, anus.

Jack and Jill (1)
Rhyming slang for contraceptive pill. Heard about the latest one for men? You put it in your shoe and it makes you limp!

Jack and Jill (2)
Rhyming slang for restaurant bill. I was at a restaurant so exclusive, you needed I.D. even if you were paying cash!

jackaroo
An apprentice stockman or cowboy working on outback properties. His female counterpart is known as a jillaroo.

jack, got the
Contracted venereal disease. (See also *flying fox*.)

jack off, to
One sure way of not getting the jack—to masturbate!

jack, to get . . . of
To lose one's patience with something or someone.

jack, to . . . up
To refuse to do something.

jake, she'll be
Everything will be all right—orright?

jaw-breaker
A long, hard, unpronounceable word or a very hard piece of lolly (candy).

jerry
A chamber pot that lives under your bed in case you need to take a slash in the middle of the night.

Jessie, more hide than
Jessie was a popular Sydney Taronga Park zoo elephant in the late 1930s and if you are brash, outlandish and bold, you are said to have more hide than her. As Jessie said to the naked man, 'How do you breathe through that thing?', or 'It's cute, but can it pick up peanuts?'

jiffy
A very short period of time. 'I'll be with you in just a jiffy.'

JAW-BREAKER

JERRY

jiggered
Something that has fallen into total disrepair or someone who is totally exhausted is utterly and completely jiggered.

Jimmy Riddle, going for a
Going to the toilet to urinate. Rhyming slang for piddle.

job, to
To punch. 'He jobbed him right on the nose.'

Joe Blakes
Rhyming slang for the shakes—generally what happens after you accidentally tread on a joey or a condition brought on by a prolonged bout of drinking (brought on by accidentally treading on a joey).

Joe Blow
Aussie equivalent of the U.S. John Doe . . . any Joe Blow will tell you that!

joey
The baby kangaroo carried in its mother's pouch. You'll know if you've ever eaten kangaroo meat when you get an uncontrollable urge to carry your kid around in your trousers!

Joey Blake
Rhyming slang for snake—sometimes referred to as joeys.

joker

Nothing to do with the game of cards (or even Batman). Just a general term used for a bloke. 'This joker came up and asked me directions.'

judge, saluting the

It's always puzzled me how racehorses don't fall over when doing this as they pass the winning post.

jumbuck

Aboriginal word for the sheep made famous in our world renowned song, 'Waltzing Matilda'.

jumper

Our word for sweater, pullover or jersey. Pathetic old Aussie riddle: What do you get when you cross a sheep with a kangaroo? A woolly jumper of course. What do you get when you cross a Christmas stocking with Dolly Parton? A thank you note from Santa!

jumper, stick it up your

A mild exclamation of rejection. You can also 'stick it up your bum'. (See also **up yours**!)

SALUTING THE JUDGE

jump, take a running . . . at yourself
    Yet another expression of rejection.

junket trumpet
    For the politically correct—the penis . . . I don't think any further elaboration is
    required, do you?

KANGAROO (THAT'S ME STUPID!)

kangaroo
The beloved symbol of Australia seen on the tail fins of all our Qantas aircraft. We also put them on our coins. We shoot them, use them as pet food, make soup out of their tails and their paws make very natty little bottle openers. Yep, there can't be a more useful national symbol than the old kanga mate!

kangaroo hopping
What your car does when you accidentally lift your foot off the clutch . . . particularly by learner drivers. My first girlfriend had a lot of trouble getting her licence—just couldn't get the hang of actually sitting up in a car.

kangaroos, keeps . . . in the top paddock
Anyone who is a bit stupid. In most areas of Australia, kangaroos are regarded as pests (even vermin) as they defoliate much grazing land.

Khyber, a kick up the
You've just been given a kick up the backside. Khyber: abbreviation of Khyber Pass (rhyming slang for arse).

Khyber, to be given the
Similar to a knockback—to be rejected or, in the case of your job—to be fired.

kick a goal, to

To either be successful in getting the woman of your dreams to make wild, passionate love to you, or to achieve success in your business endeavours. 'George kicked a goal today with the new supply contract then kicked another one with that sheila from accounts!'

kick in, to

What happens when they pass the hat around—you kick in a dollar or two. It's also referred to as kicking the tin which is what we would probably do for the relatives of someone who has just kicked the bucket.

kick on, to (1)

To recuperate or achieve success in business.

kick on, to (2)

To move on to yet another social function after the one you're at ceases. 'We went to a party at Joe's place then kicked on until 3a.m. at Harry's.'

kick, couldn't get a . . . in a stampede

Term used to describe an out-of-form footballer. Actually, at the end of each match, my team looks like they've been run over by a stampede.

kindy

Abbreviation for kindergarten—my dad used to walk me there every day . . . actually he was in the same class as me!

A KICK UP THE KHYBER

king hit

A surprise punch delivered from behind . . . but enough of my wife's remedy for my drinking and gambling habits—let's move on.

kip (1)

A short nap.

kip (2)

Used in the uniquely Australian game of two-up, the kip is the small, flat piece of wood upon which two pennies are placed and thrown into the air. Participants bet on whether the coins will come down tails, heads or odds.

Kiwi

A New Zealander—sometimes mistaken for an Aussie (as Canadians are for Americans). Kiwis however, are easily distinguished for their unusual use of vowels. E.g. Six becomes 'sux', sex becomes 'six' and flat becomes 'flet'. Therefore, if you get an invitation from a Kiwi to be at their 'flet at sux for a bit of six and fush and chups afterwards', it sounds like a reasonable sort of proposition! By the way, a kiwi is also a nocturnal New Zealand native bird.

kiwi fruit

No, not a New Zealand homosexual but a furry round fruit more commonly known as a Chinese gooseberry.

knackered (1)

Totally exhausted or totally useless. 'He was knackered at the end of the marathon.'

KIWI

knackered (2)

To have one's testicles (knackers) cut out—presumably originating from the place a lot of the horses I back finish up—the knackery!

knickers

Shorts, underpants or, more commonly, ladies' panties. When calming somebody down, a common expression is, 'Don't get your knickers in a twist!'

knife, to go under the

Quite simply, to be operated on. I suspect my surgeon wears those rubber gloves so he won't leave any fingerprints.

knock (1)

To find fault with something is to knock it.

knock (2)

Sexual intercourse.

knockback (1)

A refusal.

knockback (2)

To drink a glass of beer. 'He knocked back a beer.'

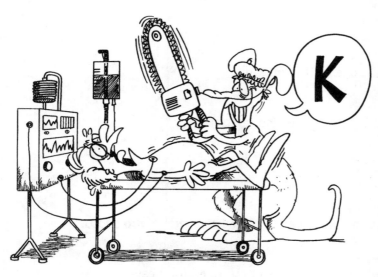

TO GO UNDER THE KNIFE

KNOCK-UP

knockdown
An introduction to a member of the opposite sex. 'I wouldn't mind a knockdown to that good lookin' sheila one day!'

knocker, on the
Exactly, spot on, bull's-eye!

knockers (1)
People who constantly find fault.

knockers (2)
A woman's breasts. (See also *norks*.)

knock-off time
Going home time after work.

knock-shop
A brothel or massage parlour. (See also *rub 'n' tug shops*.)

knocked up
If you've just made your wife or girlfriend (or, heaven forbid—both) pregnant, you have just knocked them up.

knotted, get

Polite way of telling someone to go forth and multiply.

knuckle sandwich

What you get when someone punches you in the mouth. As my dear old dad used to say, 'Remember son, the bigger they are, the harder you hit the ground!'

KNOTTED

LAIRED UP

la de da
Anyone who acts in a pretentious or snobbish manner is said to be a bit la de da. (See also **up yourself**.)

Lady (or Lord) Muck
The same person. 'Who does she think she is—Lady Muck or something!'

lair
Any chap who dresses and/or acts in a loud, boorish manner in order to attract attention to himself.

laired up
Dressed to the nines in very loud clothing.

lairise, to . . . around
Activities include doing wheelies to attract attention, singing bawdy songs, dropping your trousers etc.

larrikin
Close cousin of the lair. A young, mischievous (but generally likeable) chap.

Larry Dooley, to give someone
  To either severely berate or administer a thorough thrashing. I cop both when late home from the golf club!

lash out, to
  To go on a wild spending spree on something totally self-indulgent. 'He lashed out and bought himself a brand new set of golf clubs.'

lash, to give it a
  To have a try at something.

last shower, I didn't come down in the
  I'm not as stupid as I look mate! The fool that takes me for an idiot is no galah!

lav
  Abbreviation of lavvy—abbreviation of lavatory.
  Oh dear, what can the matter be
  Two old maids were locked in a lavatory
  They were there from Friday to Saturdee
  Nobody knew they were there!
  (Pathetic isn't it?)

LASH OUT

left footer
If you kick with the left foot, you're either of the Roman Catholic persuasion or a homosexual. Indeed, a bisexual person is said to kick with both feet. We have yet to find an expression for a bisexual Roman Catholic (but we're working on it!)

leftie
Anyone with socialist or communist leanings.

leg opener
Crude term for any alcoholic beverage that lowers a woman's sexual inhibitions. (I don't think I can put it more delicately than that ladies!)

lemon and sarse
Rhyming slang for arse . . . you can be either sitting on it—or given it. (Sarse is short for sarsparilla—a cola-style soft drink.)

lezzo
Abbreviation for lesbian . . . I think I might be one, I'm starting to fancy women!

lid, I dips me
I take my hat off to you!

life, go for your
An invitation to go right ahead with your intentions. It can also mean to move very quickly.

lippie
Lipstick—of course.

liquid amber
Quite obviously—beer.

little boys
Small saveloys (for the obvious reasons).

little house
No, not that famous one on the prairie—the one down the bottom of your backyard—the outside toilet (dunny).

liver, shit on the
In a foul mood. (See also *muck on the pluck*.)

LOLLY BOY

lizards, starve the
Rural exclamation of astonishment or exasperation. (See also **stone the crows**!)

loaf, using your
Abbreviation of loaf of bread, rhyming slang for head. Anyone using their loaf could figure that one out!

lob, to
To arrive (generally unexpectedly).

lolly
What Americans call a sweet or candy.

lolly boy/girl
Young person selling confectionery and drinks at a cinema or sporting venue.

lolly, do your
Lose your temper, go off your face, chuck a right old spaz!

lolly water
Any weak, insipid drink with little or no alcoholic kick.

London to a brick
Betting term used to indicate a sure thing. Phrase popularised by Sydney racecaller Ken Howard. A brick being a ten pound ($20) note.

TO DO YOUR LOLLY

loo, the (1)
The toilet.

Loo, the (2)
Abbreviation for Sydney suburb of Woolloomooloo (the sound made by a constipated cow!).

looney bin
Mental asylum. (See also *giggle house*.)

loop the loop
Rhyming slang for soup.

lousy bastard
A mean, niggardly person who wouldn't piss on you if you were on fire.

lousy, feeling
Not feeling very well at all.

lower than a snake's arse/belly
Anyone of low moral fibre.

lumbered, to get
To be caught in the act or arrested by the cops. 'He was climbing out the window with the VCR under his arm when he got lumbered by the police.'

lumbered, to get . . . with

To have some sort of unwanted responsibility or onus placed on you. 'He left the restaurant without paying and I got lumbered with the bill.'

lunch

Collective noun describing your landing gear—you know, your penis and testicles! Male ballet dancers bring their lunch to work every day.

lurk, on to a good

To be receiving great benefit in return for the least amount (if any) of work. Some say our politicians are on the best lurks (and perks!) of all.

luv

Term used when a bloke can't remember a woman's name. In these days of political correctness, be very careful to whom you use this form of address.

luvvie

Term used by some of my gay acquaintances when they can't remember a bloke's name!

LUNCH

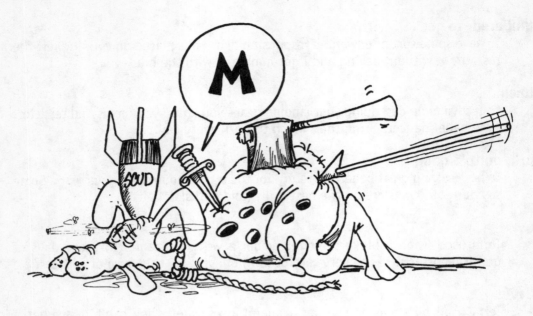

DEAD AS A MAGGOT

mad as a cut snake
Very angry, very reckless or totally stupid.

mad as a meat axe
Totally insane.

mad, he went . . . and they shot him
Infantile, pathetic excuse to cover a person's whereabouts.

madwoman's breakfast, all over the place like a
Totally confused or disorganised—but enough about me—let's move on shall we?

mag (1)
To gossip idly. 'I had a bit of a mag with Dave about the footy.'

mag (2)
Abbreviation for magnesium wheels. 'This car comes with a complete set of mags.'

maggot, dead as a
As you can see from the illustration—not in very good health, deceased, cactus!

mail, the

Very similar to the good oil. Inside information—generally heard at a race-track about a sure thing.

Mainlanders

What the good folk of Tasmania call us fellow Aussies who live on the Big Island (Australia).

makings, the

Very simply—tobacco and cigarette papers. For those of you who like to roll your own. (See also *rollies*.)

Mallee root

Rhyming slang for prostitute. Mallee roots are the large roots of various eucalypts from the Mallee region of Victoria.

Mallee root, face like a

. . . and are generally twisted and contorted. If you resemble one, you are deemed to be quite ugly—I do hope you have a nice personality but!

map, to throw a

To vomit.

mappa

Now this is a little convoluted but I'll try to explain and remember ladies, I'm just the messenger. Mappa is an abbreviation of map of Tasmania. This state, being sort of triangular in shape, is said to resemble the female pubic area—get the picture?

marble, to pass in your

To die, expire, cease to exist, to cark it!

mark, to take a

In the football game of Aussie Rules, to catch a ball after it's been kicked. In the early days of the game, when the ball was caught, the player would make a mark on the turf where he caught it and sometimes do a place kick for goal. If a player takes a mark high above the pack, he has taken either a specky (spectacular) or he's pulled down a screamer.

mate

Generally used by the male of the species when addressing a fellow male. U.S. equivalent—pal. 'Owyergoin mate, orright?'

MATINEE SESSION

Matilda

As featured in the world famous Banjo Paterson song, 'Waltzing Matilda'; it is the bedroll carried by nomadic bushmen (or swaggies) who roamed (waltzed) around Australia looking for work.

matinee session

Generally, any sexual activity carried on outside normal night-time hours. E.g. breakfast-time, lunch-time, in the car on the way to work, in an elevator, under the desk, in the lunch-room etc. These days, a matinee session for me involves just watching the midday movie on telly!

mean, so . . . that

He wouldn't give you the wind off his farts.
He wouldn't give you a wave if he owned the ocean.
He wouldn't give a rat a railway pie.
He wouldn't give a dog a drink at his mirage.
He wouldn't shout if a shark bit him.
He wouldn't give you the time of day.
He wouldn't piss on you if you were on fire . . .
That's pretty bloody mean if you ask me!

Mediterranean back

Suspect back injury feigned to avoid work and to falsely claim welfare payments. So called as it is allegedly more prevalent amongst migrant groups (although plenty of Aussies suffer the same malady!).

Melbourne Cup

The horse race that stops a nation for three minutes the first Tuesday of each November. Victoria is probably the only state in the world that declares a public holiday for a horse race.

merchant

These come in a variety of guises—there's the stand over merchant, the panic merchant, and the king-hit merchant. All experts in their particular field. Some people say I'm a bulldust merchant!

merchant banker

Rhyming slang for wanker. (See also *halfback flanker*.)

metho addict

As the title implies—a person addicted to methylated spirits. I knew a bloke who drank a whole bottle of furniture polish—terrible death . . . but a lovely finish!

Mexicans

What folk from the northern states call Victorians—because they live south of the border.

Mick

A Roman Catholic or an Irishman.

MELBOURNE CUP

Mickey Mouse
A strange one this one—it's rhyming slang for grouse (or excellent) but it can also indicate that something is a bit quirky, tricky or suspect.

Mickey, taking the . . . (or Michelle) out of
Sending somebody up. (See also *taking the piss*.)

middy
In Western Australia, a 7oz (200ml) glass of beer, and in New South Wales a 10oz (300ml) glass—I think I'll have one of each thanks!

milk bar
The distinctly Australian equivalent of the American drug store where you can buy everything from a litre of milk, to a loaf of bread, to a packet of fags.

milker, busier than a one-armed . . . on a dairy farm
Yet an-udder expression to describe a hectic situation.

milko
Distant cousin of the rabbit-oh and the bottle-oh . . . that dying breed of men who used to deliver the milk.

million, gone a
Beyond hope. Utterly and totally defeated.

miserable bastard
Someone who complains incessantly or is mean with their money (or both!).

missed by a bee's dick
In the words of Maxwell Smart, 'Missed by that much chief!'

missed by a gnat's nasty
Not that anyone's ever seen one, but even smaller than the bee's penis!

missus, the
The trouble 'n' strife, the ball 'n' chain, the cheese 'n' kisses . . . the wife!

mockers, to put the . . . on
To put a hex or jinx on somebody or something.

mockies
Abbreviation for footwear worn by fashion victims—moccasins, generally worn

with skin-tight stone- or marble-washed jeans. How tight? Well, you can actually see the outline of his vaccination scar!

mollies

Now these are a bit more fashionable. Robust moleskin trousers worn by stockmen to prevent chafing whilst on horseback. Also worn by city slickers who would like the girls to think they've got a big holding somewhere. (But we know what they're holding—don't we girls!)

mollydooker

A left-handed person—I'd give my right arm to be ambidextrous.

Mondayitis

That dreadful feeling that overtakes you at the beginning of your working week. 'George won't be in today—he's got a bad case of Mondayitis.' It is also acceptable to come down with Mondayitis on a Tuesday, Wednesday, Thursday or even Friday!

moniker

My wife's middle name (actually it's Monica) and another name for one's name and/or signature. 'Just whack your moniker on this contract and we can start doing some business.'

MONDAY-ITIS

monty

A sure thing. 'This horse is a monty to win this race.' Also used to describe inevitability. 'He was a monty to be sprung by the cops when he went through the red light.'

moosh

That big hole under your nose where the food goes in or, generally speaking, your face.

more front than Myer

Brazen, unabashed and bold. Situated in Melbourne, the Myer Emporium is the largest department store in the southern hemisphere and, as you would imagine, has a rather large street frontage.

Moreton Bay fig

Not only a magnificent tree found in Queensland, but rhyming slang for a wig.

morning glory

An erection a lot of chaps wake up with each morning—sometimes called a piss-fat. More tea Vicar?

mother-in-law's kiss, colder than a

Blizzardly freezing!

motherless

Hopeless, despairing. 'He came stone motherless last in his most recent race.'

TO HAVE MOUSETRAPS IN YOUR POCKETS

MOZZIE

motza/motser
A large amount of money—I hope to make a motza out of this book for instance.

mousetraps, to have . . . in your pockets
To be mean and miserly with your money.

mouth like a horse collar
A mouth so big, he could eat an apple through a picket fence.

mozz, to put the . . . on
Very similar to putting on the mockers. To wish failure or misfortune on someone.

mozzie
Abbreviation for the legendary Aussie mosquito. So big in some parts, they have been known to carry black box flight recorders—true!

muck
Something you step in—i.e. dog's muck or something mothers tell their daughters to get off their face if they've put on too much make-up. 'Get that muck off your face this instant girlie!'

muck in
To help out with an unpleasant task.

mucking about (1)
Simply wasting time doing nothing in particular.

mucking about (2)
If somebody is mucking about with your missus, he's certainly not wasting time doing nothing in particular—divorce lawyers at 20 paces!

muck on the pluck
In a horrible mood. (See also *shit on the liver*.)

muddie
If ever you're in Queensland try one—they make great eating—the mud crab.

mudguts
Affectionate greeting used when you meet an old friend whose name escapes you momentarily. 'G'day mudguts, howyadoin'?'

mudlark/mudrunner
Term used to describe a racehorse that runs well on a wet or heavy track.

mullet, like a stunned
To be in a confused or addled state.

munga
Food. (U.S. equivalent: grub.)

Murray, on the
Rhyming slang for betting on credit—on the Murray cod (nod). The Murray is the river that forms part of the border between the states of Victoria and New South Wales.

muso
Abbreviation of musician. The musos in our band are individual geniuses—it's just when they play together they have a problem!

muss, a ball of
Feeling extremely fit and well—a ball of muscle in fact.

my oath!
Typical Aussie exclamation of affirmation. (See also *bloody oath*.)

mystery bag

Your average sausage (or snag). So called because it was generally thought that your friendly butcher used to supplement the meat with anything else he had lying around the shop—like sawdust, sheep's eyes, bull's balls etc.

my word!

Yet another exclamation of affirmation. 'Are my mystery bags 100 per cent meat?' 'My word they are!'

myxo

Abbreviation for myxomatosis—a rather cruel and devastating disease introduced into Australia's rabbit population in order to eradicate them.

MYSTERY BAG

NAGA AWARD

NAGA award
A trophy I've won many times—an acronym for Not A Golfer's Arsehole. The last time I won a NAGA, the only two decent balls I hit all day was when I stood on a rake in a bunker!

name dropper
As I was saying to my good friend and buddy Mel Gibson the other night . . .

nana, to do your
Losing your temper—pronounced nar-nar, it alludes to doing your banana.

nappies
What·our American friends call diapers. I know a 20-year-old girl who just married an 85-year-old bloke—which is great. When they eventually have a baby, the father can share the same nappy service as the kid!

nark (1)
A spoilsport.

nark (2)

To needle, annoy or pester.

narkie

In a foul mood, short-tempered and irritable.

nasho

National service or a national serviceman.

naughty

Juvenile euphemism for sexual intercourse. Personally, I prefer to use the more sophisticated term, Mr Naughties!

neck, to go under your

To gain (unfair) advantage or gain by getting in first by dubious means.

necking it

To drink straight from the bottle. My favourite vintages? Red and white!

Ned Kelly

Infamous Australian bushranger. Anyone who indulges in dishonest, deceitful and dubious dealings is said to be a bit of a Ned Kelly. A golfer playing to par off a handicap of 27 for instance!

NAPPY

neddies, the
If you are going off to the neddies, you're planning a day at the race track. Good luck!

Never-Never (1)
Description of some of the most isolated, remote areas of outback Australia.

never-never (2)
Buying goods on credit. You never-never seem to be able to pay it off because of the 36 'easy payments' contract you just signed. I just consolidated all my 25 hire purchase contracts. Now, at the end of each month, I only have one bill I can't pay.

niagaras
You'll know if you've just been kicked in the niagaras because you will be doubled over in pain and your eyes will be watering rather profusely. Niagara Falls—rhyming slang for balls.

nicked, get (1)
A less aggressive way of telling somebody to get stuffed (or, go forth and multiply).

nicked, get (2)
If you are caught doing an illegal act by the constabulary, you have just been nicked. 'George got nicked by the cops for speeding last night and got into even more trouble when he told them to get nicked!'

nick, in good
In good condition. For instance, Jane Fonda is still in good nick for her age.

nick, in the (1)
Totally naked.

nick, in the (2)
Totally knackered—you're in gaol!

nick off (1)
What you say to someone when you are no longer in need of their company. (See also *piss off*.)

nick off (2)
To disappear. 'He nicked off from work to play a round of golf.'

niner
A nine gallon keg of beer—very popular at big Aussie barbeques.

nineteenth hole
The bar at your golf club—I always score at that one!

nit, to keep
To keep a watch out for the authorities at any illegal activity.

Noah's ark
Rhyming slang for shark . . . not too many left in Australia . . . the crocodiles have eaten most of them. True dinks!

No beg pardons
Going full bore at some activity (generally sport) with no apologies for your determination and zeal.

noggin (1)
Your head. Being resourceful is using your noggin.

noggin (1)
A glass of beer. 'Harry's gone down the pub for a few noggins.'

NOAH'S ARK

no-hoper

What my old man said I'd always be—a ne'er do well, a failure at most things in life.

non compos

Shortened version of Latin phrase, non compos mentis. To be unconscious—generally due to an over-indulgence of alcohol.

nong (1)

An idiot.

nong (2)

Your head. 'He used his nong to work it out.'

noodle

Again, your head. If you have been using your noggin, nong or your nut, you probably would have figured that out by now!

norks

Women's breasts. 'She's got a great set of norks!' I had this terrible dream last night—I dreamt Dolly Parton was my mother and I was a bottle-fed baby! (See also **knockers** and **fun bags**.)

Norm

Character from government 'Life Be In It' get-fit promotional campaign. Any lazy, layabout bloke with a pot belly who refuses to exercise has become known as a Norm.

north and south

Probably more Cockney than Australian—rhyming slang for mouth.

Northern Territory champagne

Not found on your average wine list, this rather unique little number is a subtle blend of methylated spirits and health salts. Tends to linger on the palate . . . for about ten years if you're not used to it!

nose, on the (1)

In racing parlance, backing a horse to win outright.

nose, on the (2)

Anything (or body) with a vile smell is said to be a bit on the nose. (See also **woofie**.)

nose, on the (3)

A dubious business proposition can also be on the nose. This raises a situation where someone on the nose at a racetrack advises you to put twenty dollars on the nose of a racehorse ridden by a jockey who is on the take and thus on the nose! (Sometimes my intellect astounds me!)

no worries

An expression used to instil confidence. Often used by politicians, accountants and tradesmen.

no wukkin's

Abbreviation of no wukkin' furries—a spoonerism. (Just say it quietly to yourself.)

nude nut

A follicly challenged person.

nuddy, in the

Totally naked. The most popular bloke at our local nudist colony is Harry Longfellow—he can carry two cups of coffee and six donuts—all at the same time! Nobody ever wants to eat the donuts for some strange reason.

IN THE NUDDY

OCKER

ocker

Uncultured, chauvinistic Aussie equivalent of the American redneck. Loves his sport, beer, mates and sheilas—generally in that order!

off like a bride's nightie, to be

If you recall your wedding night—this phrase relates to taking off (departing) rather quickly. I remember on our wedding night after I got undressed, my wife locking herself in the bathroom—laughing hysterically!

oil, the good

The right (inside) information.

oily rag, living off the smell of an

To be poverty stricken.

old boiler

Generally referring to a tough old chicken. Also more commonly used to describe any woman approaching middle age—with apologies to all the old boilers in my life at present (and they know who they are!).

old boy, the

The penis.

old fellow, the
The old boy!

old girl, the
Your wife or your mother.

oldies, the
Your parents (or parents-in-law). 'We're visiting the oldies this weekend.'

old man, the
Either your father or your penis—try not to get them mixed up!

one-eyed trouser snake
You could hardly call it a euphemism but yet another term for the old boy, the old fella, the old man, the blue-vein junket trumpet. Now you know why women don't have brains girls, they don't have a penis to store them in!

one brick short of a load
As we say these days—mentally challenged. You know—one chop short of a barbeque, two sandwiches short of a picnic or one grape short of a bunch etc.

once-over, to give it the
To conduct a cursory inspection of something (or someone).

one-armed bandit
Old fashioned poker machine with a handle that used to rob you of your hard earned almost as quickly as the new fangled ones!

LIVING OFF THE SMELL OF AN OILY RAG

Onkaparinga
Brand name of well-known blanket and rhyming slang for 'finger'.

on ya
Abbreviation of the term good on you—or well done!

oo-roo
A very Aussie way of saying goodbye.

open slather
Unrestrained activity—a free hand to do or say anything you like (unless of course you're a henpecked hubbie!).

optic, having an
Abbreviation of optic nerve which becomes rhyming slang for perve—the practice of lustfully leering at lassies (or laddies).

orchestras
Abbreviation of orchestra stalls and rhyming slang for balls (of the testicular variety). 'The cricket ball got him right in the orchestras.' (See also *crown* and *family jewels*.)

order of the boot
To be fired (or booted) out of your job. Just think though, this dubious honour now means that each day when you arise, you're already at work—looking for it!

ORDER OF THE BOOT

O.S.

O.S.

Yet another example of the great Aussie penchant for abbreviation. One never 'travels overseas'—ya go O.S. mate! To places like K.L. (Kuala Lumpur), F-one-J-one (Fiji), Bangers (Bangkok), Singers (Singapore) and not forgetting of course F.N.Q.! It's OK, it merely means Far North Queensland.

Oscar

Something you'll need a lot of when you go O.S.—rhyming slang for cash. Oscar Asche was an Aussie actor who died in 1936.

outback, the

The desolate heart of Australia—or, any other remote, uninhabitable, dry, inhospitable region (but enough about my wife's side of the bed!). God, I hope she never reads this far, otherwise I'm cactus.

outer, on the

To be out of favour or excluded. At a cricket or football match, non-members watch the game from the outer area of the ground where conditions are generally abysmal. It's even worse when they run outer pies and beer!

Oxford scholar

Rhyming slang for dollar. Sometimes shortened to just Oxford. 'He's made a few Oxfords out of his business over the years.'

Oz

What every red-blooded Aussie briefly calls home—Australia mate!

PACKING IT

Pacific peso

What we call our dollar whenever it drops below at least $U.S. 0.70. At least the English pound is steady—it's still only 16 ounces! (GRRROAN!!!)

packing it, shit

Terrified out of your wits. Derived from World War Two slang term 'packing death', which means trying not to poo your pants in fear when facing eradication at the hands of the enemy.

Paddo

Abbreviation of trendy inner-Sydney suburb of Paddington . . . very yuppie. So yuppie that burglars never break in if they know you're having company!

paddywhacking

No, not bashing an Irishman—it's just another term for spanking. If you're very naughty—watch out, because it'll be paddywhack the drumstick for you young man! Pretty banal eh?

pants man

An Aussie Casanova.

paper bag, couldn't fight his way out of a

A pathetic pugilist—weak as water, a wimp.

para
> Thoroughly intoxicated. Abbreviation of paralytic. So drunk, he fell asleep as soon as his head hit the accelerator!

Parliament
> (See also *giggle house, house of Reps, all yack . . . and no yakker, rathouse*.)

pashing on
> What Americans call 'necking'. Derived from (of course) the word passionate.

pasting
> A comprehensive defeat. My beloved football team has copped many a pasting over the years.

Pat, on your
> Alone. Abbreviation of rhyming slang for Pat Malone.

pav
> A deliciously decadent dessert consisting of a meringue base topped with whipped cream and fruit salad. Invented by an Australian chef and named after Anna Pavlova, the Russian ballerina who ceased answering her phone back in 1931. But remember girls, a minute on the lips—months on the hips!

pay out
> To be roundly criticised or abused. 'Jim copped a real pay out from the boss when he stuffed up the Perkins contract.'

PASH

THE RESULT OF TOO MUCH PAV

pearler
Excellent or wonderful. My wife's a real pearler . . . give me a break—she may actually read this book one day!

pelican shit, a long streak of
An affectionate (?) term for any tall, thin, rakish chap.

perk (1)
Any little extra benefits your job provides. I.e. an expense account, company car, or that cute little typist from front office, is said to be a perk. Our politicians have made perking an art form whereas we mere mortals pay a fringe benefit tax for ours.

perk (2)
To vomit. 'My baby daughter has just perked all over me!'

persuader, the
The jockey's whip.

perve
Generally a male pastime of leering lustfully at lasses with a lascivious longing. However, in these politically correct days, it's now permissible for you girls to do it to us blokes . . . but do try and control yourselves ladies!

physio

Abbreviation of physiotherapist—which, as you can see, has six syllables. We have deliberately shortened it to three so our sportsmen (footballers in particular) can pronounce it . . . only gaggin' guys!

piano player in a brothel, he's just the

Phrase used to describe someone oblivious to what's going on around him. Funny, I thought they only dealt with organs in brothels!

Piccadilly

Rhyming slang for chilly. 'It's a bit Piccadilly out this morning.'

piddle

To take a piddle is to urinate.

piddling

Small, insignificant and petty—which is how I'm described by blokes standing beside me taking a piddle!

pigs!

A shortened exclamation of disbelief or disparagement. Extended versions include: pig's bum! pig's arse! or in a pig's eye!

pike out

To go back on one's word or back out of a deal or arrangement.

PIANO PLAYER IN A BROTHEL

piker
Someone weak of heart or spirit. 'C'mon Harry, don't be a piker—jump into this icy cold swimming pool!'

pimp
As well as a prostitute's minder, a pimp is also someone who tells tales on you. (See also **dob**.)

pineapple, to cop the rough end of the
To be the recipient of a raw deal. Come to think of it, the other end of the pineapple would probably make your eyes water just as much!

pinko
Anybody with leftist or socialist political leanings. Derived from the colour used to signify communism . . . may it rest in peace!

pip, giving one the
To needle or anger someone is to give them the pip. (See also **irrits**.)

piss (1)
Urinate.

piss (2)
Euphemism for alcohol. 'Harry really got on the piss last night, in fact, he got pissed as a parrot.'

pissing in someone's pocket
Insincere flattery and/or sycophancy. For example, if I was to tell you that you have shown great literary judgement in buying this book and recommending it to all your friends—I'd be pissing in your pocket.

pissing it up against the wall
Wasting all your money on drinking.

piss, taking the
Being sarcastic towards someone, or telling them what an unmitigated failure they are.

piss up, couldn't organise a . . . in a brewery
Obviously someone whose organisational skills are a little wanting.

Pitt Street farmer

The New South Wales equivalent of a Victorian Collins Street farmer. Both streets are financial hubs and the farmers are blokes who buy rural properties purely for investment and wouldn't know one end of a cow from another.

pixies, away with the

Sometimes also alluded to as being 'away with the fairies'—it simply means to daydream or to be unrealistically optimistic. 'If Bob reckons Elle Macpherson rang him for a date last night, he's definitely away with the pixies!'

plate, bring a

If a host or hostess asks you to 'bring a plate', it doesn't mean they've run out of crockery—it's a quaint Aussie custom of bringing a plate of sandwiches to a social function to help ease the catering costs.

plates of meat

Rhyming slang for feet. Big ones look a bit like plates of meat.

plonk

Really cheap wine—ancient Aussie mythology has it that to manufacture this wine, you simply throw a bunch of grapes into the air and they come down 'plonk'.

O.K, I'LL TAKE YOUR WORD FOR IT... ITS COLD!!

COLDER THAN A POLAR BEAR'S BUM

poet's day
Aussie term for Friday. A great tradition in this country is manufacturing our own, individual longish weekends, hence we: Piss Off Early—Tomorrow's Saturday!

poke
Sexual intercourse. 'Jim went to the disco and managed to pick himself up a poke (willing female) for the night.'

poke a stick at, more than you can
An over-supply or abundance of something—politicians for example!

poke in the eye with a burnt stick, better than a
Expression used to indicate you haven't got exactly what you wanted but you'll make the most of what you do have. I hear this expression a lot when my wife talks to her mother (and mine!) on the phone.

polar bear's bum, colder than a
Not that anyone has ever survived sticking a thermometer up there but, I would imagine, pretty bloody cold! (See also *Mother-in-law's kiss, colder than*.)

pole, up the
In a confused state or acting illogically.

pole, wouldn't touch it with a forty foot
Something or someone very dubious—to keep well away from.

pollie
A politician. Our local member is amazing, when there's nothing left to say—he's still saying it!

Pom/Pommie
Affectionate Aussie term for person of British extraction. We think the term originated from P.O.M.E. (Prisoner of Mother England), from the convict era and later shortened to POM.

pong
A nauseous odour. Or, figuratively speaking, if something seems a bit dubious, it is said to have a 'bit of a pong about it'.

pony (1)
For the light drinker, a very small glass (about half) of beer.

PONG

pony (2)

In our old currency (pounds, shillings and pence), 25 pounds or $50.

poofteenth

Used to denote a very small distance. 'Just move a poofteenth to your left so I can focus', said the photographer.

poofter

Uncomplimentary term for a male homosexual. In Australia however, you don't have to be one to be called one. A rival sinking a ten metre putt to win a golf game or an Aussie Rules umpire paying a dubious free kick can legitimately be called poofters as well.

poo, in the

In either financial trouble or just simply in any sort of strife.

poor, so . . . he's licking the paint off the fence

Poverty stricken. My family was so poor, I had to wear hand-me-downs to school—which was very embarrassing having only two sisters!

porcelain bus, driving the

Here's how you do it: get on your knees in front of the toilet, firmly grasp each side of the bowl (as you would a steering wheel) . . . now, start throwing up. Congratulations! You are now driving the porcelain bus.

pork and bean
Male homosexual—rhyming slang for queen.

port
Term used principally in Queensland and New South Wales to describe a suitcase. Abbreviation of portmanteau.

posh
Anyone of seemingly refined taste and impeccable breeding brought about by an abundance of wealth. Thought to have derived from the days when the rich sailed on magnificent ocean liners and would demand, 'Portside out—starboard home.'

possie
It's essential you get a good one at the footy so as not to miss any of the action. Abbreviation of position.

possum, stirring the
Deliberately causing trouble by mentioning the unmentionable in order to get a response . . . these days it's simply called 'stirring' and perpetrated by stirrers.

postie
Quite simply, the postman (mailman).

pot (1)
In Victoria and Queensland, a large (300ml) glass of beer. If you drink enough of them—you'll very quickly develop one of these . . .

pot (2)
A very large beer belly! My mate, huge Hughie, hasn't seen his feet for twenty-five years!

potted, to get
To fall pregnant.

pox doctor's clerk, dressed up like a
To be attired in cheap, gaudy clothes. 'Hey! Nice threads you're wearing—it's a pity someone's made them into such a bad suit!'

prang
A car smash. (See also *bingle*.)

prawn
> What Americans call a shrimp. We have some of the biggest and best prawns in the world. So big in fact that one of them ate my dog when he was swimming at the beach . . . true!

preggers
> Pregnant, in the pudding club, up the duff . . .

prezzies
> Gifts—corruption of 'presents'.

prick and ribs, all . . . like a drover's dog
> Very lean, sinewy and ready for action. I've been likened more to a drover's corgi!

proppy
> Term used to describe the way a footballer limps just after being slightly injured (but not enough to be taken from the field—you have to lose a leg before *that* happens in Oz!).

proverbial, up the
> A less offensive way of saying 'up shit creek without a paddle', or to be in trouble. 'Proverbial' is often used in place of bodily parts as well. 'He copped one right in the proverbials.'

pub crawl
> Literally, to visit as many hotels as you can in one day, getting progressively pissed as a parrot—ancient Aussie custom.

pudding club
> Congratulations—you're pregnant!

pull your head in!
> Just another way of telling someone to mind their own bloody business.

pup, the night's a
> The night has only just begun.

put in, to (1)
> To do your fair share of the work or make that extra effort in sports activities.

put in, to (2)
> To inform on (or dob in).

put one over, to
> If someone has put one over you, they have just tricked or deceived you. If I told you this book was a literary masterpiece, I would be putting one over you.

put up job
> What the Brits would call a 'fit-up'. A contrived situation designed to deceive.

QANTAS

Qantas

The only 'Q' word in the world not followed by a 'u'. That's because it's an acronym for Australia's international and domestic airline, originally the Queensland and Northern Territories Air Service. Pronounced 'kwont-arse', it is sometimes also pronounced 'quaint-arse' (but only by the comedically challenged).

quack, the

The doctor. I was at my quack's the other day. I told him I couldn't fill the specimen bottle. He told me to pass it around the waiting room!

queer street, in

Sorry, nothing to do with San Francisco or the Gay and Lesbian Mardi Gras—to be on this street is to be totally bereft of funds—stony-broke in fact.

quid

Former slang term for the Australian pound note (now a two dollar coin) still in use today. 'Sorry, George is not home—he's out earning a quid for the family.'

quid, not the full

Mentally deficient. About 18/6 in the pound or, in today's currency, about $1.85. The same bloke who keeps kangaroos in the top paddock—you know, the light's on but nobody's home etc.

QUID

quilting, to cop a
To have the living suitcase belted out of you.

quince, getting on your
Someone is irritating you.

Quist, Adrian
Rhyming slang for pissed (very drunk). (See also **Adrians**.)

quoit/coit
Not only those little rope rings you chuck around on the QE II deck butt (sic) the thing you sit on . . . no, not the deck chairs silly—your anus!

TO COP A QUILTING

ABOUT TO COP A RABBIT KILLER FOR SHOUTING
"RABBIT-OH!"

rabbit-killer
> Karate-type blow to the back of the neck. Used by old time bushmen to quickly kill wounded rabbits and very handy at the drive-in, girls, to ward off those over-enthusiastic dates.

rabbit on
> To talk non-stop about nothing in particular.

rabbit-oh
> The chap who used to wander around your neighbourhood selling freshly killed rabbits yelling 'Rabbit-oh!'. Near relation of the 'bottle-oh'.

racehorse
> A very thin roll-your-own cigarette.

race off, to
> The act of seducing a member of the opposite sex and racing off for some spontaneous fornication.

rack off
> Another expression for scram, go away, piss off, nick off etc.

rag
> An inferior newspaper of little or no substance.

raincoat
> Euphemism for condom—from the view that wearing one is a bit like taking a shower with a raincoat on.

raining, if it was . . . pea soup, he'd only have a fork
> An expression of misfortune.

raining, if it was . . . tits, he'd come up sucking his thumb
> Same unfortunate chump!

rap, a big
> High praise . . . I'm hoping the critics will be a big rap for this book for instance.

rapt
> To be totally infatuated with someone (or thing) is to be rapt.

rash, all over him/her like a
> The state of not being able to keep your hands off someone. I know a guy who has that problem with himself!

ratbag
> An eccentric of diminished responsibility.

RACK OFF AND RATBAG

rat, cunning as a shithouse
As this phrase suggests—very shrewd and not to be trusted.

rathouse
A lunatic asylum and sometimes a description of parliament.

rat, like a . . . up a drainpipe
Taking full advantage of a situation. Sexually speaking, not waiting for a willing female partner to have second thoughts about you.

rat, like a . . . with a gold tooth
Insincerity personified.

rat's arse, doesn't give a
Doesn't really care one iota.

rats on sticks
Most owners hate the expression and hardly ever use it when referring to their greyhounds.

rattletrap
Any old car that rattles a lot.

raw prawn, don't come the
Expression used to tell someone you are not as stupid as you look and are not easily duped, deceived or deluded.

RAZZ

razoo, not a brass

To not have a brass razoo is to be totally broke. A razoo is a gambling chip.

razz

To mock or deride someone who has left themselves vulnerable.

RBT

Random Breath Testing—generally carried out at the roadside by cops manning 'booze buses'. Not a good idea to tell the officer you're only driving because you're too pissed to walk.

reccy

Abbreviation of reconnaissance. You could be doing a reccy of an area for a film shoot or doing a reccy around a dance floor to see what's on offer.

Redfern, getting off at

Coitus interruptus. Redfern being a railway station just before Central, Sydney's main terminus. These days I don't even make it onto the train!

red hot

Over-priced, outlandish, totally unreasonable. 'They charged us $200 to get into Barry Manilow's concert which we thought was a bit red hot!' No offence Bazza!

GETTING OFF AT REDFERN

red rattler

Old style red-painted wooden Victorian trains. So-called because they were very draughty and extremely noisy.

reffo

Seldom used term from post World War Two days for refugee.

Reg Grundys

Rhyming slang for undies (underpants). Reg Grundy is Australia's best known quiz and game show producer. I'm still awaiting a response to my latest idea—celebrity nude baked bean wrestling! Obviously Reg must be very busy at the moment.

rego

No, not the aforementioned Reg's Irish cousin, but simply an abbreviation of car registration. 'This is a quality motor with 8 months rego left on it!'

rellie

Abbreviation of relative—as in aunt, uncle etc. Sometimes called rello.

Repat, the

As any ex-serviceman knows—the repatriation hospital.

Reps, House of

Not the reptile enclosure at your local zoo (although a cynic would argue otherwise) . . . it's the Lower House of Federal Parliament—the House of Representatives.

Red Heads

Popular brand of matches with a red-headed woman on the box. Until recently, manufactured in Australia by Bryant & May but now fully imported.

rev head

Close relative of your petrol head.

revolving door, couldn't go two rounds with a

A pathetic wimp.

Rice, a roll Jack . . . couldn't jump over

A huge wad of money. Jack Rice was the name of a champion equine hurdler. (I think he might have been a horse as well!)

rice, couldn't knock the skin off a . . . pudding
Close mate of the guy in the revolving door.

Richard, the
Totally useless or exhausted. 'You might as well throw away this saucepan with a hole in it—it's had the Richard (or Dick)!'

ridgie-didge
Just another way of saying 'fair dinkum'. A description of anything that is a straight up, genuine article.

right-oh
Another way an Aussie says OK. Sometimes we even lengthen it to 'right-ee-oh'. (See also *rotary hoe*!)

ring
Your anus. (See also *freckle*, *dot*, *bronze* and *acre*.)

ringer
The fastest shearer in the shed—so called because he runs rings around all the others.

ring wobbler
Any racehorse that causes wild fluctuations in the betting ring.

ripper
Exclamation of surprise or delight. 'I've just won the lottery—you little bloody ripper!'

ripper bonzer
An extension of ripper.

rip-roaring
Anything loud or tumultuous—we Aussies are very fond of a rip-roaring booze-up.

ripsnorter
Yet another adjective to describe something exciting or pleasing. 'I went to a ripper of a party last night, had a rip-roaring time, met this ripper bonzer sheila who turned out to be a real ripsnorter!'

roaring trade
If your business is going well, you are said to be doing a 'roaring trade'.

roaring-up, to cop a
   To receive a severe tongue-lashing.

robber's dog, head like a
   Generally used to describe an unattractive female . . . we are talking mega flea collar here chaps!

rock and roller
   A Rolls-Royce motor car.

rocket
   If you cop a rocket from your boss, you receive a harsh dressing down. Rockets can also come from your missus—I get so many from mine, I've nick-named her Exocet!

rocking horse poop, as rare as
   Well, when was the last time you stepped in any? A very scarce commodity.

Rock, the
   Arguably, Australia's best known landmark and the largest monolith in the world—Ayers Rock. Situated in the Northern Territory not far from Alice Springs, the Aboriginal name for it is Uluru. (Plurry big yonnie!)

ROBBER'S DOG

AS RARE AS ROCKING HORSE POOP

rollie

A hand-made cigarette—a 'roll your own'.

'ron, keep one for

When botting a cigarette, a professional will always ask for another for 'ron, i.e. later on.

roo

Abbreviation of kangaroo.

roo bar

No, not a kangaroo with an erection or where they drink . . . it's the metal frame fitted to the front of your car to fend off our furry friends when driving through the bush or the outback.

root

In America, you sit in the grandstand and root for your team. If you did the same thing in Australia, you'd probably get arrested because having a root in Australia means having sexual intercourse. It is not only a verb (doing word) but can also be used as a noun. 'Harry's girlfriend turned out to be a top root!' (Sorry ladies, just being expansive!)

rooted

Either totally useless or totally exhausted . . . we tried to warn you Harry!

rort

> A deceptive scheme designed to manipulate the system. Receiving welfare payments under false pretences is said to be 'rorting the system'.

rotary hoe!

> Corruption of term 'right-oh' or 'OK'.

rotgut

> Inexpensive (dirt cheap) nasty wine that does to your stomach exactly what the name implies.

rotten, to get

> To become inebriated.

roughie

> A long-priced racehorse (or a slovenly woman).

row, to go for a

> To have a mishap—like falling over or being charged with an offence. 'Bill went for a row when the cops caught him doing 180 kph . . . in his own driveway!'

R.S.

> Used to describe how you're feeling or anything of an inferior nature. Initials for 'rat shit'—which is about as low as one can go . . . or feel!

GETTING ROOTED BY A RUN-IN WITH A ROO BAR !

rubbity
Short for rubbity tub or tub—rhyming slang for pub.

rub 'n' tug shop
Brothel masquerading as a massage parlour.

rug-rat
A toddler or small child.

Rules
Abbreviation for the greatest game on earth (biased Victorian speaking)—Australian Rules football.

run-around, getting the
When someone is deliberately avoiding you, fobbing you off or feeding you misleading information—you are copping the old run-around.

run-in
A confrontation or a quarrel. 'Bill had a run-in with his missus last night after getting home late from cards.'

rust-bucket
A car riddled with rust—in fact the only thing holding it together is the paint!

GREAT AUSTRALIAN SALUTE

sack, to get the
> Is to be fired from your job.

Sallie
> Any member of the Salvation Army—also referred to as Salvos. Little known fact—there has never been a Salvation Navy!

saloon passage, to get a
> Racing parlance for a horse getting an unimpeded run. Derived (we suspect) from nautical expression for rich passengers booking a saloon passage on a luxury liner.

salute, the great Australian
> The waving motion constantly made by the hands to ward off the ever-present and extremely persistent Aussie blowie (blowfly).

sambo
> Wait! Before you report me to the racial vilification police—it's merely the abbreviation for a sandwich.

sandgroper
> A native of Australia's biggest and richest state, West Australia—home of the West Coast Eagles Aussie Rules football team.

ONE SANDWICH SHORT OF A PICNIC

sandwich, one . . . short of a picnic
The same bloke who keeps kangaroos in the top paddock and wonders if his sister has a baby girl—does that make him an aunt or an uncle!

sanger
Another term for a sandwich.

sarky
Short for sarcastic.

sausage, not worth a
Pretty bloody useless really.

sausage roll (1)
Piece of sausage meat (which can be anything from four to 18 centimetres—that's one-and-a-half inches to seven inches long—in the old money) wrapped in pastry in the shape of a sausage. Delicious hot and dipped in tomato sauce.

sausage roll (2)
Australian Rules football rhyming slang for goal. (See also *sosso*.)

sav
Abbreviation for saveloy (savoury sausage). Also known as little boys—for the obvious reason!

sav, fair suck of the
Exclamation demanding fair play. (See also ***fair suck of the sauce bottle***! and ***fair suck of the sausage***!)

sav, sink the
Sexual activity involving penile penetration—as if it needed explanation! Also referred to as 'sinking the sausage or soss'.

saver, have a
To cover a bet by backing another horse—generally in the same race.

school
A group of mates taking turns to buy drinks in a pub is known as a 'school'.

schooner
Common to New South Wales, a 425ml (15 oz) glass of beer. In South Australia its equivalent is 255ml (9 oz).

scoot, on the
If you are on the scoot, you're on a drinking spree.

scoot, to
To depart. 'Must scoot—goodbye!'

PULLING DOWN A SCREAMER

scone
> You really didn't need to use your scone (head) to work that one out didja?

scorcher
> A very hot day or a very hot date.

scorpions, to have . . . in your pockets
> To be very mean with your money—really professional niggards also keep mousetraps and death-adders in there as well.

scream blue murder, to
> To whinge or complain loud and long.

screamer (1)
> A good looking girl who is very free with her favours.

screamer (2)
> Whenever an Aussie Rules footballer leaps high above the pack and catches (marks) the ball, he is said to have just pulled in a screamer. Later that night, he will probably go to a disco in the hope of pulling in yet another screamer (1) who may have seen his screamer on the television replay!

scrounger, an old
> Used to describe old men who look through rubbish bins etc for food or anything else of value . . . I just hope they don't come across any copies of this book!

scrub, the
> Aussie term for the outback or rural areas. 'We're going up the scrub for our holidays this year.'

scrubber
> Untidy, unattractive girl of questionable morals.

scunge (1)
> Untidy, unkempt, unclean person who doesn't care how they smell or look . . . in fact, they look quite scungy.

scunge (2)
> To borrow (bot) something with no intention of repaying the favour is to scunge. 'This derro just scunged a fag off me!'

scungies

Extremely brief male swimming costume. To impress the girls at the beach, try wearing a potato down your scungies. The first time I tried it, they all ran off screaming. Then someone told me the potato actually goes down the *front*!

seen more pricks than a second hand dartboard

Obviously, a very promiscuous woman (or bloke—let's not be too sexist now!).

semi (1)

In Australia, we pronounce it 'sem-ee' and it's a house attached down one wall to another (semi-detached).

semi (2)

Also pronounced 'sem-ee' and it's an abbreviation of semi-trailer or articulated vehicle. My cat got run over by a semi. I know cats are supposed to have nine lives—but the semi had eighteen wheels!

send up

To satirise or mock.

septic (1)

An American. Abbreviation of septic tank—rhyming slang for Yank.

septic (2)

Amongst my circle of friends—masturbation. Let me explain; septic tank is rhyming slang for wank.

serve, to cop a

To be severely admonished or criticised. 'Wilbur copped a real serve from the boss for arriving late this morning.'

settler's clock

So called because it starts laughing just before dark, the kookaburra (laughing jackass).

shag (1)

To be forsaken or totally deserted is to be left like a shag on a rock. A shag being a rough mass of hair or a crested cormorant.

shag (2)

Yet another euphemism for sexual intercourse. Typically tender Aussie mating call: 'How about a shag, hag?'

TWO SHAGGiN' WAGONS

shagger's back
> Malady allegedly brought on by too much shagging! (We are not alluding to the crested cormorant here.)

shaggin' wagon
> Now, how does that bumper sticker go? 'If this wagon's rockin'—don't come knockin'.' In Australia, a panel van equipped with a mattress and surround sound stereo, designed exclusively for the purpose of copulation—until such time as you leave home and get yourself your own apartment.

shaggledick
> Affectionate term used to greet someone who is quite familiar but whose name you've forgotten. 'G'day shaggledick—can I buy you a beer?'

shaking hands with the wife's best friend
> Urinating—pathetic isn't it girls!

shandy
> The forerunner of light beer—a mixture of beer and lemonade . . . I think I'm gunna throw up!

shat off, to be
> To be fed up or totally despondent about something or someone. (Shat being the past tense of shit, as any grammar expert will tell you.)

sheila
> Woman or girl—we've got the grousest sheilas in the world here in Australia.

shellacking
> A severe beating—either in sport or in a back alley!

she'll be right
> Reassuring expression meaning 'It'll be OK'. (See also ***she'll be jake*** and ***she'll be apples***.)

sherbet
> In Australia, when we say we're going out for a couple of sherbets—we are actually going out for a couple of beers.

shickered
> What happens to you after too many sherbets . . . drunk as a skunk!

shingle, one . . . short
> Mentally challenged—one shingle short of a roof.

shiralee
> Another name for the rolled up blanket containing a swaggie's (tramp's) worldly goods. Also known as a swag.

SHEILA

shirt-front
A heavy, front-on tackle in football. The first time the recipient sees it coming is days later on the television replay of the incident at the tribunal!

shirt-lifter
A male homosexual.

shirty
Annoyed or in a very bad mood—especially after being shirt-fronted by a shickered shirt-lifter! (I just love alliteration—don't you?)

shitcan
To soundly criticise or rubbish something is to shitcan it. I just hope the critics don't shitcan this book too much.

shit creek, up . . . without a paddle
In deep trouble (or doo doo!).

shit-hot
To be excellent at something. 'Allan is a shit-hot batsman.'

shits, cracking it for the
To become very annoyed.

shitty
What you become after getting very annoyed.

shoot through, to
To decamp hastily—generally after not paying your debts. (See also *shoot through like a Bondi tram*.)

short and curlies
If someone has got you by the short and curlies—it's simply another way of saying they have you by the balls. In this case however, we can use the expression with no gender bias whatsoever.

shot, take a . . . at
Either making an attempt at something or, in the Australian idiom, passing a sarcastic or inflammatory remark.

shot, that's the
Exclamation of approval.

shouse
Strine for outside lavatory (shit-house) or anything inferior.

shout
When it's your turn to buy the drinks, it's your shout. I know a bloke who is so mean—he wouldn't shout in a shark attack!

shrapnel
Loose change.

shrimp
What we call very small prawns or very wimpy people.

shut the gate
Expression used when your team has an unbeatable lead. 'After Fitzroy kicked their fortieth goal against Collingwood (I wish!) in the first quarter, from there on in, it was shut the gate.'

sick canary, couldn't knock the dags off a
Obviously, that's the way Collingwood were playing that day—very weak.

sickie
A day taken off work due to illness (imagined or otherwise). Sickies taken either on a Monday or a Friday are generally regarded with great suspicion.

silly as a two bob watch
Well, you couldn't really take a 20 cent watch seriously, now could you?

silly as a wheel
All the same attributes as your two bob watch.

sin bin
A panel-van used for the specific purpose of fornication (generally at the drive-in). I still take my wife to the drive-in and, when the movie is over, I go back there to pick her up!

sink the sausage, to
Obviously—to copulate!

sink the sav, to
To sink the sausage!

siphon the python, to
> To urinate. (See also ***draining the dragon***.)

six o'clock swill
> Old timers will remind you of the days when pubs used to close at 6 p.m.— causing a mad rush (swill) for drinks just before closing. These days, it's almost a 25 hour swill (that's if you drink for the hour it takes you to get home!).

six of the best
> Used to discipline recalcitrant schoolboys. Six strokes of the leather strap across the palms of the hands. (I still have the scars!)

skerrick
> A small amount of nothing. 'There wasn't a skerrick of food in the fridge.' I worry whenever I find an empty plate in ours—I get to thinking something in there must have eaten what was on it!

skid-lid
> Slang term for crash helmet.

skinful, had a (1)
> To be totally inebriated.

skinful, had a (2)
> To be totally fed up with someone. 'I've had a skinful of you today—get out!'

skinner
> The bookies' friend. A long-priced winner that effectively skins the long-suffering punter.

skint
> Totally broke (too many skinners!).

Skippy
> Slang term for Aussie (from popular Australian television series).

skite
> To skite is to brag or show-off.

sky rocket
> Rhyming slang for pocket . . . which now explains where the term 'pocket rocket' comes from!

slacker

A malingerer.

slag, to (1)

To spit.

slag, to (2)

To criticise or make derogatory remarks. 'The boss is constantly slagging off at the way I do my work.'

slash, taking a

Urinating.

slather, open

No holds barred!

sledging

Mainly prevalent in cricket, it's the act of making insulting and provocative remarks to your opposition. Things like: 'Hey is that your real face or are you just breaking it in for a clown!' or 'Your mother smells like a camel!' Pretty aggressive stuff eh!

sling, copping a

Receiving an illicit payment, bribe or bonus.

SLEDGING

sling off at, to
To make hurtful, derogatory remarks about someone.

slipper, sinking the
Literally (or figuratively) to kick someone during a fight.

slops, on the
To be on a drinking binge is to be 'on the slops'. Can anyone tell me which bourbon goes best with chardonnay?

slug, to
To overcharge. Oft seen headline in Australia: 'Massive Tax Slug Likely'.

sly grog shop
Now extinct since six o'clock closing was abolished, a shop selling liquor out of hours without a permit.

smaller, the . . . the property, the wider the brim
A truism used to demonstrate that just because you look prosperous, you may not be able to come up with the goods when required. Close cousin of wanker. A bit like having a champagne diet on a beer income.

smart Alec
Near relation of a smart arse—a know-all.

smart arse
Knows Alec!

smasher
A person (generally female) who is very attractive. 'Annie is a real smasher of a sheila!'

smell, hanging around like a bad
Making a general nuisance of oneself by not knowing when one's company is no longer desirable.

smoko
Now that smoking has been banned in most buildings, workers can be seen everywhere these days outside on the pavement puffing away during their smoko.

snag
A sausage. (See also *mystery bags* and *sossos*.)

WENT FOR A CRAP AND THE
SNIPER GOT HIM

snakey
> In a nasty, foul mood.

snatch
> Female genitalia.

snip, to
> To catch someone in a vulnerable state of mind and borrow money that they would never normally lend to you. 'That bludger Colin just snipped me for ten dollars!'

sniper, went for a crap and the . . . got him
> A lame-brain excuse used in the military to cover someone's whereabouts.

snowing down south, it's
> Your petticoat's showing—in my case, it's leg dandruff!

soap, wouldn't know him from a bar of
> A totally unrecognisable person.

so hungry I could eat the crutch out of a low flying duck
> Here, have one of my sandwiches instead!

S.O.L.
> To be in an unpleasant frame of mind—'Shit On the Liver'. (See also ***muck on the pluck***.)

sook
A wimp or cry-baby—generally used to describe children or politicians who fail to get re-elected and whinge and complain about it.

sort, a good
An attractive female (or male).

soss, hide the
Sexual intercourse—as in 'hide the sausage'.

sosso
A sausage (or penis). We suggest you don't barbeque or prick the latter!

soul-case, work the . . . out of
To toil long and hard for very little money or appreciation—all the women I know call it housework!

suitcase, to bash the living . . . out of
A polite way of indicating a severe beating. What we're really trying to say here is: 'He had the living shit punched out of him.'

spag (1)
Abbreviation of spaghetti.

spag (2)
And, because spaghetti comes from Italy, it's also a derogatory term for a person of that ancestry.

speed merchant
A fast driver.

Speedos
Almost generic brand name of swimming costume for men and women.

spider
Any soft drink with a dob of ice-cream floating on the top—heaven!

spinebashing
The art of lying flat on your back in bed—asleep!

spinner, come in (1)
Call made to person tossing two-up coins once all bets are laid and the ring is clear.

spinner, come in (2)
Derisive expression used to indicate to someone that you've just duped or made a fool of them.

spit
What you do when you get angry—you 'spit it'. As in 'spit the dummy' or 'spitting chips'.

spit, to go the big
To vomit.

splash the boots, to
To urinate.

sponger
Close relative of the bludger—someone who never pays, relying mainly on the efforts of others.

sport
Another way of addressing someone instead of using the term 'mate'. 'G'day sport—howyadoin, orright?'

sprog (1)
A child.

SPRUNG

sprog (2)
Semen.

spruiker
Loud person standing outside or inside a department store or sideshow extolling the virtues of the wares within.

sprung
What happens when your husband comes home to find you in a tryst with the TV repairman. You have just been 'sprung'.

spud
A potato.

spunk (1)
A good-looking bloke or sheila (depending on your preference!).

spunk (2)
Almost obsolete term for semen.

squib
A cowardly person inclined to shirk an issue or situation rather than confront it.

squiz
A quick look. 'I'll just take a quick squiz at this report before the meeting.'

stack
A collision in a motor car. 'Norm just stacked his car into a tree.'

stack on a turn, to (1)
To cause a commotion or throw a tantrum. (See also: *wobbly, chuck a*)

stack on a turn, to (2)
To throw a party—and you have every right to 'stack on a turn' (1) if you don't get invited!

starkers (1)
Totally, stark raving mad.

starkers (2)
Totally, stark raving naked!

starve the lizards!
Exclamation of astonishment.

steak and kidney
Rhyming slang for the beautiful city of Sydney—capital of Australia's most populous state and home of the 2000 Olympics!

stick
Affectionate term for a male or female. 'That Johnny Blackman's not a bad stick!'

sticker licker
South Australian term for a parking officer . . . unfortunately, a protected species!

sticks, the
Any rural area.

sticks, the big
Aussie Rules goal posts.

sticky tape
As the name suggests, tape you use on parcels etc. We sometimes call it Durex (brand-name) which really amuses the Poms as they have a brand of condom carrying the same name—the latter is less painful to remove after sex!

STICKER LICKER

stiff cheddar
> An expression indicating bad luck.

stiff cheese
> Even more bad luck—sometimes used: hard cheese.

stiff, to be a bit
> As they say in the classics, 'You don't have to be dead to be stiff!' To be unlucky.

stiffy
> An erection—and we don't mean a building!

stirrer
> A trouble-maker—derived from shit stirrer and stirring the possum.

stone the crows!
> Yet another exclamation of astonishment. (You can also exclaim 'starve the crows!')

stonkered
> Exhausted.

stretcher case
> Football term for any victim of a shirt-front.

strewth!
> Another exclamation of astonishment. 'Strewth! Didja see that bloke get shirt-fronted just then?'

strides
> Trousers (or daks).

strike a light!
> Yet another in a long line of exclamations of astonishment.

strike me pink!
> Yes folks, anothery just like the othery!

Strine
> In some respects, what this dictionary issorlabout. The unashamed lazy corruption of English as she is spoke. Strine being our lazy way of saying

Australian . . . (Or-Strine!) in our own unique dialect.

Stubbies
Brand-name of male shorts which are almost de rigeur on a hot day around the barbeque or in the bar of your local pub.

stubby
Short, rotund little bottle of beer.

stuck, get . . . into (1)
To tackle a task with gusto and enthusiasm or ....

stuck, get . . . into (2)
To either physically or verbally assault someone. Hence, one could have a situation where your missus gets stuck into you for not getting stuck into weeding the garden.

stuck pig, to squeal like a
To moan or complain loud and long.

stuck-up
Aloof, conceited. (See also *up yourself*.)

stuffed (1)
Very tired or exhausted.

stuffed (2)
Anything that is beyond repair or totally useless is deemed to be stuffed.

stuff-up
The Aussie equivalent of the American screw-up and the British cock-up. (See also *balls-up*.)

stumps (1)
The three wooden sticks found at either end of a cricket pitch. The aim of the game is for the bowler to hit them and dislodge the two little bits of wood perched on top of them (the bails).

stumps (2)
The end of your working day. Derived from cricket when they pull stumps at the end of a match or after a day's play. 'OK boys—it's five o'clock. Let's call it stumps for the day.'

subbie

Term often used in the building trade for a sub-contractor.

suds

Beer.

sunbeam

Any piece of crockery or cutlery that doesn't need washing up at the end of a meal. Our dishwasher broke down recently—so I offered her more housekeeping and she cheered up immediately!

sundowner

Swaggie (tramp) who generally arrives at your homestead at sundown. Just a little too late to do any work but just in time for a meal. I've got a few mates in the city who work this scam just as well!

sunnies

Sunglasses.

super

Abbreviation of superannuation. My grandfather went broke when he retired after investing all his super in developing the ten kilogram hand grenade!

suss

Anything or anyone of dubious origin is regarded as a bit suss (suspicious).

SWALLOWING THE ANCHOR

sussed

Discovered doing something you shouldn't!

suss it out, to

Means simply to check it out. If it proves to be OK it has been sussed out. I just hope those literary critics don't suss me out before we go into reprint!

swag

What wandering bushmen (swaggies) carry all their belongings in. A rolled-up blanket.

swallow the anchor, to

What old salts do when they give up their seafaring days. My great-uncle Horatio was a bit of a lady's man back in his nautical days—in fact, he had an inflatable girl in every port (it saved an awful lot of alimony!).

sweet Fanny Adams

Expression meaning nil, zero, nothing. Also a less offensive way of saying sweet f.a. (fuck all).

swifty, to pull a

To dupe somebody.

swipe, to

To steal.

swipe, to take a

To either attempt to punch somebody or to pass a derogatory or sarcastic comment about them.

sword, had the

If something has had the sword it has become totally useless. (See also **had the Dick/Richard**.)

swy

More commonly known as the distinctly Aussie gambling game (played in all our casinos and regarded as one of the fairest forms of betting)—two-up. The game involves throwing two pennies in the air and betting on whether they fall heads, tails or odds.

T.A.B.

ta
Thank you! (You're welcome.)

T.A.B.
Initials of our government-run Totalisator Agency Board betting shops. I backed a horse the other day at 20–1. Unfortunately it came in at around 20 past 4! (Groaning permissible here!)

tack, flat
Extremely rapid (unlike that stupid nag).

tack, flat as a
How I felt after backing that stupid horse—depressed and despondent.

Taffy
Any native of Wales.

tailor-mades
A cigarette that comes in a packet that you don't have to roll yourself.

talent, checking out the
A male or female pastime that can be indulged in just about anywhere. The perennial search for that perfect partner at a pub, club, disco, beach or restaurant. Remember fellas, if she can open a six-pack with her toes—marry her!

talk, he/she could . . . under wet cement
Now we all know someone like this—don't we?

Tallarook, things are crook in
Inane phrase indicating an adverse situation.
Others include: Things are weak at Julia Creek, Got the arse at Bulli Pass, There's not much lucre in Echuca, . . . but the good news is . . . The girls are dandy in Urandangie!

tan track merchant/bandit
A male homosexual.

tarp
Abbreviation for tarpaulin.

tarting-up
Either putting on far too much make-up or superficially embellishing something to make it appear more appealing. E.g. A building, a car or even a body!

tart plate
With apologies to the fair sex—the pillion seat on a motorbike. Little wonder these male chauvinist biking pigs only ever get to throw their leg over a Harley eh girls?

TART-PLATE

ta ta
Goodbye! Young children sometimes go ta tas (on a trip) to grandma's house.

taxidermist, go see a
Go and get stuffed!

tear-arse
Anybody fond of always travelling hastily is said to be tear-arsing around and hence is a tear arse.

tearer of bollicles
Something or someone outstanding or pleasing. Variation on ball tearer. (Bollicles = testicles!)

technicolour yawn
To throw up. I don't imagine you need any elaboration on this one.

telly
Abbreviation (of course) for television. We were watching telly last night and my wife said 'God this is boring!' I said, 'If you think this is boring, wait 'til I turn it on!'

GIVING A THICKHEAD A THICK EAR!

thick as two short planks

Not very bright at all. The sort of person who wonders where all the mistakes go when they rub them out!

thick ear

The result of a cuff around the ears. Often preceded by the question, 'How would you like a thick ear mate?!' Thickheads generally answer yes!

thingummybob

Descriptive (?) term for anything that's very complicated and beyond the comprehension of mere mortals. 'I think it's the thingummybob where the spark plugs go in' said she to the mechanic.

thingummyjig

What the mechanic fixed the thingummybob with!

threepence, able to turn on a

Indicating a car or sportsperson with a very tight turning circle. For our younger viewers, a threepence (in the old currency) used to be worth about three cents—these days, it's not worth a pinch of cocky's poop!

throw a leg, to

Male expression for sexual intercourse (romantic eh!). Another expression is 'get the leg over'.

thumbs, a handful of

Extremely clumsy.

thunder box

An outside or inside lavatory . . . the name says it all!

tick (1)

A very short moment in time. 'I'll be with you in a tick.'

tick (2)

Credit. 'I don't have any money at the moment—would you mind putting it on tick until payday?'

tickets

To have tickets on yourself is to be extremely conceited . . . the sort of person who rings Dial-A-Prayer to ask if there are any messages.

tick off
> A very stern scolding or rebuke. 'His wife gave him a good ticking off for getting home late from the pub.'

tiddly
> Just slightly intoxicated.

tiger for punishment
> Anyone with an almost masochistic desire to be treated badly or exploited.

tight-arse
> A miser.

Tijuana, to be given the
> To be either fired from your job or scorned and ignored. Abbreviation of Tijuana brass—rhyming slang for arse.

tin-arse
> No relation to Mr Tight-arse but simply someone who always seems to be very lucky.

tinnie
> A blizzardly cold can of beer. One of the great Australian rituals—crackin' a tinnie with a mate! Very blokey indeed.

AS USEFUL AS TITS ON A BULL

tinny

A blood brother of Mr Tin-arse. People forever having good fortune are said to be tinny.

titfer

Probably Cockney in origin—abbreviation of tit for tat—rhyming slang for hat.

tin tack (1)

Rhyming slang for your back.

tin tack (2)

Rhyming slang for the sack (to be fired). Probably for spending too much time off work on your tin tack!

tits on a bull, as useful as

A bit like me in the kitchen—totally useless!

toe, a bit of

Sorry, nothing to do with foot fetishists! If your car can suck the doors off the one beside it from a standing start, it is said to have a bit of toe (or poke).

toey, a bit

Eager, apprehensive, ready and rarin' to go. A footballer, a racehorse, me on my wedding night!

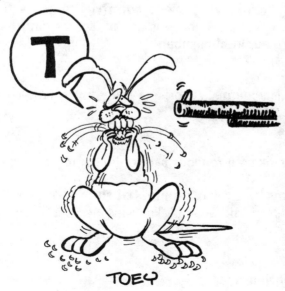

TOEY

togs
What we Aussies call a swimming costume. My mate wears his togs so brief and tight you can not only tell his sex but his religion as well!

top-off
Someone who tattle-tales on another. Very similar to a dobber.

toss, arguing the
Pointless debate after the argument has been all but resolved.

towie
A tow truck operator. Because it's such a competitive vocation, the best towie is a toey towie!

town, go to (1)
To get very angry. 'She really went to town on him.'

town, go to (2)
An expression of assent. 'Here I am girls—go to town!' Most of them thought I meant catch a bus into the city—and they did!

tracking square
What the Yanks call dating . . . going steady.

train, couldn't . . . a choko vine over a country dunny
Totally lacking in ability. A choko is one of Mother Nature's most boring vegetables—next to our local member!

trammie
Native only to Melbourne, Victoria—a tram driver. (The conductors are called connies.)

tram, on the wrong
Following a mistaken, erroneous path or line of logic.

tram, wouldn't know a . . . was up him 'til the conductor rang the bell
Vague. Same person who wouldn't know his arse was on fire 'til the fireman put the ladder up!

trannie (1)
Abbreviation of transistor radio.

trannie (2)

In photographic circles, abbreviation for transparencies—but you saw through that one didn't you!

trap for young players

A warning to the young, inexperienced and naive—generally quoted after you've totally screwed up your entire life.

traps, to go around the

Checking regular sources of information or to conduct regular inspections. Derived from rabbit catchers checking their traps for deceased bunnies.

tray

Pre-decimal term for threepenny bit.

trick, can't take a

Constant misfortune—always seemingly mocked by irony.

trifecta

Racing term used to described anything that happens in threes. E.g. He cracked it for the trifecta—she's a nymphomaniac, she's rich and she owns a pub! Crikey! That's more like a quadrella!

trimmer, you little

Exclamation of delight. A trimmer can also be a pleasing car or woman.

GO AROUND THE TRAPS

triss
> An effeminate male or homosexual.

troppo, gone
> Either moved domicile to the tropical north of Australia or suffering dementia brought on by too much heat (and possibly red rum!).

trot
> You can have either a good or bad one of these. If you've been ill for months, you're having a bad trot. If you're making lots of money, you're having a good trot!

trots, the
> But even people making a lot of money can suffer these—diarrhoea!

trouble 'n' strife
> Rhyming slang for wife.

true blue
> Trustworthy, genuine, fair dinkum.

true dinks
> Exclamation of reassurance. (Corruption of fair dinkum.)

TROTS

tube, to suck on a
  To drink directly from a can (tube) of beer.

tucker
  Food.

tuckerbag
  A swaggie's food bag—of course!

tummy banana
  The penis—also known as the tummy sausage.

turd burglar
  Male homosexual.

turf it out
  To discard something is to turf it.

turn it up!
  Exclamation demanding fair play or indicating disbelief or cynicism.

turn-up for the books
  Probably originating from racing parlance for when a long-priced horse would win and be a turn-up for the bookies, it is now used to describe any unlikely or near impossible occurrence. Like me playing off scratch before I'm fifty for instance!

turps, on the
  To be drinking any sort of alcohol . . . even turpentine!

tweeds
  Men's trousers.

twig
  To twig on to something or somebody is to suddenly gain an understanding. By now you should have twigged to the fact that you're getting close to the end of this tome!

two bob
  Pre-decimal 20 cent (two shilling) piece.

two bob each way, to have

To be indecisive, to sit on the fence or to hedge one's bets. Bisexuals are also described as having two bob each way. (That's if Bob doesn't mind!)

two-bob lair

Cheap, loudly dressed person.

two-bob watch

As you would imagine, something inferior or inefficient. 'My car's running like a two-bob watch at the moment.'

two-pot screamer

A person with a low alcohol tolerance who generally is screaming drunk after only two pots of beer.

two-up

A distinctly Aussie form of gambling involving the spinning of two pennies into the air and betting on whether they land heads, tails or odds. Played in all Australian casinos and illegally for years (two-up schools) in back lanes and deserted warehouses. (See also *swy*.)

U-EE

U-ee, doing a
Either doing a U-turn in your car or making a radical change of opinion.

ugly as a hatful
Full extension of this phrase is 'ugly as a hatful of arseholes'. Definitely not a pretty sight!

um-ah
Shamefully, almost an integral part of the Australian language. Used to fill in the gaps of a conversation while we're trying to think of what to say next. Politicians are renowned for their umming and ahhing!

umpie
In Aussie Rules football—the umpire. Despised by players and spectators alike, these much-maligned miscreants endure insults and abuse that would be devastating to a lesser mortal. (In N.S.W. rugby league—it's the ref.)

umpteenth
An infinite number . . . and if I've said it once, I've said it for the umpteenth time!

underdaks
Underpants or boxer shorts.

UGLY AS A HATFUL

underground mutton
Rabbits. (Apologies to Bugs!)

unemployed, looking down on the
Urinating . . . actually, mine's been unemployed for so long, it just qualified for emergency relief! (I've gotta get a new writer!)

up a gumtree
In a hopeless situation—stranded.

up a wattle
Either stranded or totally mistaken. Holding the wrong end of the stick!

uphill, pushing shit . . . with a sharp stick
Well, you try it! Any pointless, difficult task.

up the duff
Well and truly pregnant. If you've ever wondered how painful childbirth can be, try this little experiment suggested by my wife (and mother of our daughter). Gripping your top lip with both thumbs and forefingers, pull it out as far as you can . . . is it starting to hurt? Good—now peel it back over the top of your head! I surrender!

up the mighty ....!
Ancient Aussie war chant—simply insert the name of your favourite footy team.

UMPIE

up the spout (1)
    Totally destroyed or obliterated.

up the spout (2)
    Which is what you'll be when her father finds out you got his daughter pregnant!

UNDERDAKS

up who, who's . . . and who's not paying the rent?
World War Two expression enquiring as to who is in charge.

up yours!
Vulgar retort meaning 'up your bum/arse'. U.S. equivalent: screw you!

up yourself
Snobbish and conceited.

up yours for the rent!
Yet another dismissive exclamation reinforced by the fact that he's not going to pay his rent either!

ute
A small, open-backed truck. Abbreviation of utility. U.S. equivalent: pick-up truck.

UP THE DUFF

VEGEMITE

Vandemonian
Derived from the state of Tasmania's original name—Van Diemen's Land. Does that mean if a Tasmanian is causing trouble, it's Vandemonian pandemonium?

vaseline valley
Sorry, not a ski resort but the unflattering term used to describe the gay area of Oxford Street, Sydney.

vee-dub
Sometimes described as looking a bit like a pregnant pasty, abbreviation of 'vee-double-u'—a Volkswagen.

Vegemite
Trademark name of a black yeast extract which we Aussies use as a spread on toast and sandwiches. To the uninitiated and gourmands with sophisticated and delicate palates, it looks and tastes a little like bitumen! However, we love it because, according to Kraft, the manufacturers, 'It puts a rose in every cheek.' Vegemite also received international recognition when it became part of the lyrics of the hit song, 'Down Under' by Men at Work.

THERE'S A LIGHT ON THE VERANDAH
BUT NOBODY'S HOME

vegies
  Vegetables.

verandah, there's a light on the . . . but nobody's home
  The appearance of some intelligence but ....

verbal diarrhoea
  Anyone who talks incessantly and finds it hard to stop has a bad case of this disease. I talk to my plants a lot—my wife says it makes great fertiliser!

VERBAL DIARRHOEA

WALLOPER

wacker

An idiotic nerd.

wag (1)

A good-natured person always willing to do anything for a laugh.

wag (2)

Aussie word for 'truant'. I never wagged school, although, as you can see from this book, I was away the day they did grammar!

wake-up, to be a

To be on your guard and aware that you are about to be duped. 'I'm a wake-up to your little game, mate!'

walkabout

Aboriginal activity dating back to the Dreamtime when they would go walkabout for miles in search of food or to attend ceremonial business. Today, if you're daydreaming or have gone away on a trip with no particular destination in mind, you've 'gone walkabout'.

walk-up start

A push-over or anybody easily conned. It can also mean getting a break on your opposition.

WALTZING MATILDA

Walla Walla, to be further behind than
At an almost impossible disadvantage. Despite insurmountable handicapping, Walla Walla was a pacer who won many races.

walloper
Derogatory term for a policeman.

Waltzing Matilda
The name of our unofficial national anthem. Waltzing your Matilda comes from the early days when a swaggie (bushman) would spend his days wandering (waltzing) the countryside with all his worldly possessions wrapped in a blanket (Matilda).

wanger
The penis.

wanker
A wanger is most essential to this person—a masturbatory braggart of limited or no ability.

war paint
Women's cosmetics—used to procure male scalps.

Warwicks

Abbreviation of Warwick Farm (a Sydney racecourse) and rhyming slang for arms. On hot days, we all tend to get a little Alma Shetty (sweaty) under the War-wicks.

wash-up, the final

From the gold-mining era—the end result.

waster

An idler. (See also ***bludger***.)

Watsons, to bet like the

Betting aggressively. Originating from noted gamblers, the Watson brothers.

weak as piss

Used to describe anything insipid or a cowardly, ineffectual person.

wee wees

Infantile expression for urinating. Of course, us more mature blokes go to 'toy toys' for a 'pee pee' don't we!

wellies

An English expression we also use in Oz for Wellington boots. We tend more to call them gumboots or gummies.

A WANKER

wello

Sexual intercourse. Let me explain: Wello is an abbreviation of Wellington boot which is rhyming slang for 'root' which, as you read earlier, is another term for sexual intercourse!

welter, making a . . . of it

Taking excessive advantage of a favourable situation.

Werribee duck, to be in more shit than a

To be in deep trouble. Werribee Sewage Farm is found in Victoria with an abundance of bird life. Please don't mention the smell—Werribee residents are very sensitive about it. Whenever you drive through, just pretend someone's opened their egg sandwiches in the back seat!

whacko!

Nothing to do with Jacko! It's an exclamation of delight. If we're particularly elated, we extend it to 'whacko-the-diddly-oh'!

whack up

What bank robbers do with their loot and your family does with sandwiches on a picnic—they divide up or share equally what they've got. When my ex-wife and I whacked up our property, all I got was custody of the goldfish!

whale into

To physically assault. 'He whaled into him with a baseball bat.'

wharfie

Obviously, a wharf labourer or stevedore. One wharfie I knew was nicknamed 'the judge'—he was always sitting on a case!

wheelie

The totally pointless exercise of spinning your wheels vigorously enough to attract attention to yourself and to wear out tyres in about half the time. (You can tell this former hoon is getting old can't you!)

whinger

An incessant complainer. (See also *wife, mother- in-law*!)

whip around

A spontaneous collection of money for a departing workmate or a good cause . . . like a departing workmate for instance!

whiskers, a punch in the
Unflattering term for sexual intercourse. (See also **bearded clam, spearing the**.)

white lady
I don't suggest this be put at the top of your cocktail list: a mixture of methylated spirits, a dash of boot polish and just a pinch of iodine. Shake vigorously, then drink—continue to shake vigorously until you pass out or the ambulance arrives.

white, the man in
In Aussie rules football—the umpire. These days we have seven of them—three central, two boundary and two goal . . . and even then they still can't get it right! (Biased Fitzroy supporter speaking.)

whizzer
Male or female genitalia. Often heard around city construction sites and strip shows—'Show us your whizzer!'

whizz off
To depart rather hastily.

whopper (1)
A gigantic lie.

whopper (2)
A very loud fart. I got sacked from my job at Hungry Jack's for dropping a whopper behind the counter! (God I love that joke!)

wife's best friend, shaking hands with the
Urinating—although these days, they're just passing acquaintances! (Just a joke dear.)

wobbly, to chuck a
To throw a tantrum or lose control. Sometimes called 'chucking a spaz' (spastic).

wog
Indefinable germ that is one of the most common causes of sickies (sick leave) in Australia today. It's also an offensive term for anyone hailing from (in the main) Italy or Greece. Consequently, it's quite acceptable to tell everyone in the office that you weren't in yesterday because you were laid up in bed with a wog. Of course, the office comedian always yells out—'What was his name?' Oh my poor sides—please do not split.

wombat

Description of male Casanova. So called because, like the wombat, he eats, roots, shoots and leaves.

wonky

Dazed and unsteady on one's feet.

wood duck

Used-car salesmen love this breed of customer. They come into the caryard kicking tyres, slamming doors with money falling out of their pockets. Like picking off wood ducks at a shooting gallery!

wooden spoon

Trophy awarded for the dubious honour of coming last. Wanna see my collection?

Woodser, Jimmy

A bloke drinking alone in a pub. (See also *flies, drinking with the*.)

wood, to have the . . . on

Knowing your opponent's weaknesses and using them to your advantage.

woofers

Dogs.

WOOLLOOMOOLOO UPPERCUT

woofie
Smelly, on the nose—particularly under the arms.

Woolloomooloo uppercut
A kick to the testicles. I know a bloke who lost one of his like that. The doctors replaced it with a pickled onion and now, every time he passes a fish and chip shop—he gets an erection! (Remind me to burn my joke book please.)

woolly woofter
I don't know whether this is in regular use yet as it's only recently I've heard a mate use the term when referring to male homosexuals. Rhyming slang for poofter.

Woop Woop
A non-existent part of Australia used to describe any remote location. 'He lives a long way away—out the back of Woop Woop somewhere.'

working off a dead horse
Working purely to repay a debt.

worm burner
In sport, particularly cricket, golf and football, any ball that inadvertently skids across the ground at worm level.

worries, no . . . mate
The laconic attitude that makes Australia such a great place to live—and where procrastination is almost a virtue—is summed up by the phrase 'No worries mate!'

wowser
Any puritan who neither drinks, smokes nor has any lascivious thoughts. You know, the sort of person who looks like they're constantly sucking on a lemon.

wrap, to give a big . . . to
To extol the virtues of something or somebody.

wrestling, open air
What Aussie Rules fans call rugby league. Also called thugby, cross-country wrestling and mobile wrestling. Rugby fans call Aussie Rules aerial ping-pong!

write-off
When you bingle your $2000 car and sustain $2500 damage. Geez, one $50 parking ticket will do that to mine!

✕

x-out

To rid yourself of something or somebody. To erase it from your memory.

YABBIE

yabber
Idle chatter.

yabbie
Australian crab-like crustacean found mainly in freshwater creeks and dams. Great eating!

yachtie
A yachtsman, of course!

yack, all . . . and no yakker
All talk and no work (yakker being another word for work as in 'hard yakka', as you will see further on). (See also *Parliament*.)

yack, having a
You can do this over the fence or over a beer—having a chat, chinwag or gossip. (See also *fat, to chew the*.)

yahoo
Loud, obnoxious, uncouth lout. Wherever they go, they almost always herald their arrival with a shout of 'Yahoo!'

Yakka
Well known brand name of Australian made, heavy duty and hard wearing overalls and work clothes. Also another variation of hard work.

YARNING

Yank tank

Any large American car.

yap

Idle chat or gossip. 'We just sat around the barbie yapping all afternoon.'

yarning

Telling long, drawn out stories and reminiscing together.

Yarra (1)

The much maligned river that flows through Victoria's capital, Melbourne. Because of its murky brown colour, it's the butt of many jokes—such as, 'It's the only river in the world that flows upside down' or, 'Scientists ran some tests on it recently and found traces of water!' Very funny indeed.

Yarra (2)

A really stupid person (but no reflection on the character of the Yarra River). Origin stems from a mental asylum that was situated at Yarra Bend, Victoria.

yike

Yikes! It's a yike! Call a cop! A yike being a really serious disagreement or physically violent argument.

yobbo

Close relative of the yahoo and the American red-neck. Easily identified by their loud voice, limited social graces and huge beer belly. Generally found in areas where they let just about anyone in . . . so long as it's got a pulse and walks upright!

YARRA

yonnie
>   Small pebble or stone ideal for chucking or skimming across water.

youse
>   Pronounced 'yewse'—it's the word a lot of Aussies use to indicate more than one person. 'I'll see youse all later!'

yow, to keep
>   To keep watch.

YARRA

ZONKED

zack
> Pre-decimal currency sixpence. (Now the five cent piece and, for any golfers reading this, the ideal ball marker!)

zack, not worth a
> Worthless article or person not worth even five cents!

zed
> The way we Aussies pronounce the 26th letter of the alphabet. Hey, give me a break—there's hardly any 'zed' words left in our language!

zizz
> A short nap—derived from those little zzz's you always see in comic strips.

zonked
> Totally exhausted.

zoo, like feeding time at the
> Expression used to describe the unholy mob-like rush made for the food and drink at any social function.

Z-z-z-z-z

Which is what I am now doing after completing what I hope will be yet another literary triumph.

Thank you for buying this book. Part of the proceeds will go towards some very important delicate plastic surgery for my mother—she's been called 'sir' for the last time!

Goodnight!

FEEDING TIME AT THE ZOO